Deaths, Disasters & Dastardly Deeds in the North East

by Lorna Windham

Ralph Hedley's illustration showing a young man claiming 'Sanctuary' at Durham Cathedral.

Previous page: Durham Cathedral's Sanctuary Knocker. This is a facsimile and the 12th century original is in the Cathedral's Treasures Exhibit.

Copyright Lorna Windham 2013

First published in 2012

Reprinted and revised in 2013 by

Summerhill Books
PO Box 1210
Newcastle-upon-Tyne
NE99 4AH

www.summerhillbooks.co.uk

email: summerhillbooks@yahoo.co.uk

ISBN: 978-1-906721-55-8

Contents

Acknowledgements

I'd like to extend my sincere thanks to Newcastle Central Library for their efficient service; Picks Publishing for pointing me towards Leifchild's 1842 report; super sleuth John Gallon who always manages to put flesh on the bones of information I give him, I can't thank him enough; Jill Forster for her 'gold nugget' research in Australia; Jim and Val from Jiva for their generosity and suggestions; Linda Jenkinson for her wonderful books; Yvonne Young for her time, effort and photographs; the teams Cutts and Orechoff and Siegl and Windham for their photographs; Charles Gardiner at Northern Lines for graciously allowing my writing to be seen and heard; Ruth Henderson for listening; Steve Urwin for offering great writing opportunities; everyone at the following: Silverlink at North Shields, The Lamplight Arts Centre at Stanley, The Waddy at Durham, The Cumberland Arms at Byker, Pink Lane, Newcastle, Inhouse Writers at Morpeth, the RNA Border Reivers and SSWAG for being so encouraging and supportive; Byker Books for giving me a writing platform; New Writing North for being there; Judith Green of Search and Sue Harrison and Andrew Fletcher of Newcastle Libraries, for inviting me to talk about my writing; the Davison family for kindly allowing me to tell their story; Paul Davison for his invaluable research; the helpful staff at Blyth Cemetery Office; Malcolm Teasdale for allowing me to use one of his wonderful paintings; Wendy Breckon, who is an inspiration; my publisher Andrew Clark for believing in me; David for being David, and my family for giving me the space and time to write.

Also by Lorna Windham
Crime and Punishment in the North East

Introduction

Whilst undertaking historical research for my previous book, *Crime and Punishment in the North East*, I unearthed numerous deaths, disasters and dastardly deeds buried in ancient books and documents.

Death is one of the last taboos. We don't like talking about it and most of us live our lives as if it is never going to happen to us or our loved ones. Those who lived centuries before us were less removed from death as it was a persistent threat. Death could come by accident or murderous design; repeated invasions meant constant danger; those with differing religious beliefs to that of the established church were executed and minor offenders suffered capital punishment.

Disasters are on a grander scale, they're overwhelming events which kill or injure large numbers of people and remind us of the fragility of life. Caused by nature or man, they can occur anytime, anywhere and their effects can be beyond our wildest imaginings.

Just as man has always had the propensity to commit courageous and honourable acts he has the ability to commit dastardly deeds. Deeds that are: cruel, cowardly and wicked, whether during riot, war, rebellion or peaceful times.

This book is about people in the North and their struggle to survive against the odds.

www.lornawindham.co.uk

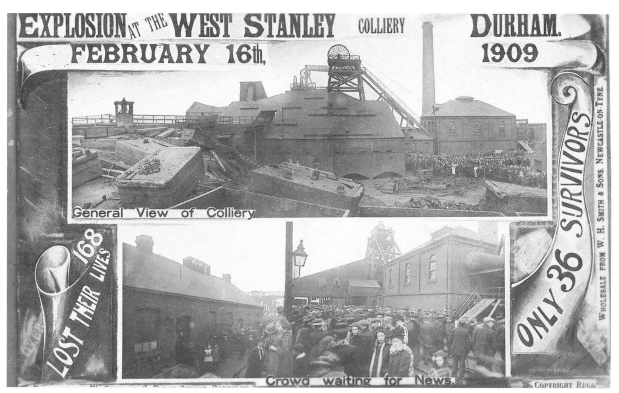

Death and disaster were common fears for the miners of the North East. Here a 'disaster card' remembers the West Stanley Colliery explosion of 1909 when 168 men and boys lost their lives.

Section One – Deaths

An unfortunate truth is: we're all going to die. Most of us would probably prefer to pass away in our own beds, but some people were not allowed that luxury.

The dead and sick travelled in style in the Jarrow ambulance.

Executions

England and Scotland have lived in relative peace since the Act of Union in 1707, but before this there was considerable unrest, and raids by both sides.

Duncan and Macbeth are famous because of Shakespeare. The real historical characters were different. Duncan was a young King of Scotland and according to contemporary historians showed poor leadership skills. For example in revenge for Northumbrians attacking Strathclyde in 1039, Duncan attacked Durham in 1040 and committed his cavalry against the city walls. The defenders used their own cavalry to counter-attack. Duncan lost the battle and some of his forces were captured.

Execution Row

Duncan's foot soldiers were slain or taken prisoner and the survivors fled the field. The captured Scottish leaders were beheaded and their heads displayed around Durham Market Place.

Duncan lived to fight another day, but a year later he was betrayed and killed by his own men commanded by Macbeth who reigned successfully for 17 years.

It is accepted as read that men die in warfare, but during centuries of religious persecution many died for their beliefs.

Durham Market Place is medieval in origin. However, the present Market Square is mainly Victorian.

Martyr Matters
October 16th, 1555

Nicholas Ridley came from a prominent northern family and grew up at Unthank Hall, near Haltwhistle, Northumberland.

Educated at the Royal Grammar School in Newcastle and then Pembroke Hall, Cambridge, he became a fellow and later Bishop of London.

When Edward I, only son of Henry VIII, died, Ridley made some serious errors of judgement which were to cost him his life. As Senior Proctor of Cambridge University, he persuaded the university to declare that the Bishop of Rome had no more authority than any other foreign bishop.

Ridley also helped Cranmer, another Protestant, to write the Book of Common Prayer; signed the letter patent giving the throne to Lady Jane Grey and preached a sermon where he declared the princesses Mary and Elizabeth were bastards.

This didn't endear Protestant theologian, Ridley to Elizabeth or her sister Catholic Mary. Once Mary was Queen, he was sent with others to the Tower and then to Bocardo Prison in Oxford.

Fifty-five year old Ridley was convicted of heresy and sentenced to be burnt at the stake in front of Baliol College, Oxford with his Protestant friend 75 year old Hugh Latimer. Latimer, born in Thurcastone, Leicestershire, was a fellow of Clare College, Cambridge. Known affectionately as 'Old father Latimer' he was a former Bishop of Gloucester and Worcester.

On October 16th, 1555, Ridley dressed in slippers, a black fur gown and velvet cap and Latimer, wearing a handkerchief, hat and old woollen coat walked to the place of their execution. The friends embraced, knelt, prayed and were forced to listen to a fifteen minute sermon by a Dr. Smith, *'Though I give my body to be burnt and have not charity it profits me nothing.'*

Ridley gave clothing and other items to the watching crowd. Latimer had nothing of worth to give, he said, *'Shall I wear my belt?'* Ridley

Bocardo Prison was by St. Michael at the Northgate and the church tower contains the martyrs' cell door.

answered, *'It will cause you more pain if you keep it, besides it will do a poor man good.'* Latimer threw his belt to the waiting hands. A smith secured a chain to their waists and the executioner hung a bag of gunpowder round their necks and lit the fire. Latimer's famous words rang out, *'Be of good courage master Ridley and play the man, for we shall this day light such a candle by God's grace in England, as I trust never shall be put out.'*

As the flames started, Ridley said, *'Lord into your hands I commend my spirit; Lord receive my spirit.'* And Latimer followed with, *'O Father of Heaven, receive my soul.'*

Latimer died quickly, but unfortunately the green faggots on Ridley's side of the stake burnt much more slowly. Ridley's brother-in-law tried to make his death speedier, but the flames only burnt Ridley's lower body.

The Church of England has always regarded Ridley, Latimer and Cranmer as martyrs for supporting its independence from the Catholic Church. They were three of over 280 people to die because of religious intolerance during Mary I's reign.

The Martyrs' Memorial outside Baliol College, Oxford commemorates the deaths of Thomas Cranmer, Nicholas Ridley and Hugh Latimer.

Mary I (1553-58) was known as '*Bloody Mary*' because of the executions of Protestants that took place during her reign. However, Elizabeth I (1558-1603) was concerned about Roman Catholics in league with Spain; plots such as Babington's to put Mary Queen of Scots on the throne followed by, in 1588, the threat of invasion by the Spanish Armada. This led to increased persecution of Catholics.

During Elizabeth I's reign, Catholic propaganda, organised by an ejected Oxford Don, William Allen, was printed in England and new English Catholic priests, trained in a seminary founded at Douai, France in 1568, flooded into England.

In 1569 the Catholic Northern Earls revolted; a year later Pope Pius V excommunicated Elizabeth I and other heretics in England and two years after that Catholics murdered thousands of Protestants in the St. Bartholomew's Day Massacre in France. These three events caused the intensification of persecution of Catholics in England.

In 1585 an Act was passed forbidding Roman Catholic priests on pain of death, to come to or remain in England. Elizabeth I meant it.

The priests would have been hanged, drawn and quartered and several executions were carried out in Durham, Gateshead and Newcastle.

Persecuted Priests

On May 27th, 1590, four Catholic priests were executed at Durham. Richard Hill, John Hogg and Richard Holyday were born in Yorkshire, whilst Edmund Duke came from Kent.

Poor Jon Speed, a layman, was executed in Durham on February 4th, 1594, not for being a priest, but for aiding and assisting them.

On August 9th, 1600, Catholic priest, Thomas Palasor, John Talbot and John Norton were apprehended in Norton's house. Norton and Talbot were convicted of aiding and assisting Palasor and they were all executed at Durham.

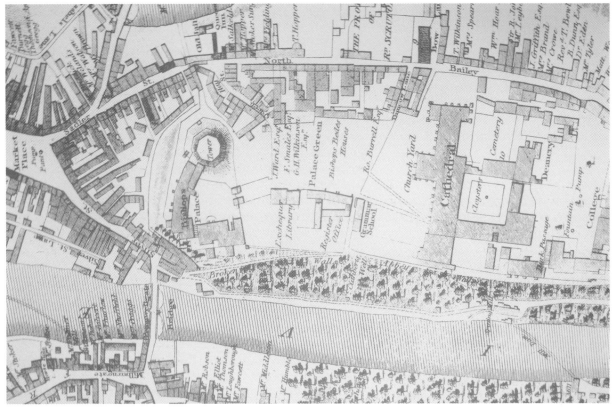

An 1820 map of Durham showing the Cathedral, Palace Green and ancient streets.

On January 7th, 1593, Edward Waterson, a Catholic priest from London was executed at Newcastle, followed seven months later by Joseph Lampton from Malton, Yorkshire.

Two Catholic priests were executed on July 24th, 1594. Jon Bost/Boast from Penrith died at Durham and Jon Ingram from Warwickshire died at Gateshead.

In the period between 1581 and 1588 at least 64 priests, 18 laymen and 2 women were executed for harbouring priests in England.

Religious persecution and superstition went hand in hand. For centuries Jews across Europe were treated as scapegoats. It is equally shocking that in the Middle Ages approximately 50,000 women were also persecuted. Accused of generating famines, plagues or anything else that went wrong, they were hanged, drowned or burned as witches. The north was as superstitious as anywhere else. Apart from the execution of Newcastle's sixteen witches and one man (a wizard) on the August 21st, 1650 (See *Crime and Punishment in the North East* p.30, Summerhill Books), there are several accounts of supposed witches who were also executed in the north. The village of Hart, near Hartlepool as well as Stockton, Gateshead and Durham have such examples.

Wicked Witches

July 28th, 1582 – Law unto Herself

In the Hart parish register, Allison Lawe is described as a, *'notorious sorcerer, and enchanter.'* She was sentenced to stand once in Durham Market Place and once in Hart and Norton churches, *'with a papir on her head.'*

Janet Allison and Janet Bainbridge from Stockton were also accused of, *'asking counsel.'*

1649 – A Witch's Grave

'Paid at Mrs. Watson's when the justices sate to examine the witches, 3s. 4d; for a grave for a witch, 6d; for trying the witches, £1 5s.' (Gateshead parish book)

January, 1652 – Witch Hunt

Two witches, Frances Adamson and Powle were found in the city of Durham and executed.

You can only feel sorry for any 'wise woman' who attempted to heal the sick or was unpopular with her fellows. Most people would try to defend themselves against injustice, however, some didn't.

Pressing Matters

There were numerous ways to execute someone involved in a serious crime. Inquisitorial questioning was used against *'heretics'*. If they remained mute it was assumed they were guilty and, *'pressing'* was used. Heavy stones were slowly placed on top of an individual's chest until they made a plea or suffocated.

In the United States of America a person accused of a crime can plead the Fifth Amendment to individual questions; this dates back to 1791 as part of the Bill of Rights. It means an individual has some protection from inadvertently incriminating him or herself and offers some protection against government interference.

England has the 1689 Bill of Rights, but it still doesn't address an individual's right to remain silent, though it does state that punishments shouldn't be unusual or cruel. In modern courts, silence could have an adverse effect on the defence. Sixteenth century churchmen in England judged a suspected convert's silence unacceptable and they tortured prisoners to persuade them to speak .

John Lambert (first called Nicolson/Nicholson) born in Norwich and educated at Queen's College, Cambridge, was the first person recorded to have objected to this type of questioning of religious beliefs. He stated that it was illegal to force men to accuse themselves. He was convicted on suspicion of having converted to Protestantism and burnt at the stake at Smithfield, London on November 22nd, 1538.

In 1563, John Foxe's famous *Book of Martyrs* about persecution of English Protestants was published. In the 16th and 17th centuries it was second only to the Bible in popularity. Why? It shone a bright light on the injustices of religious procedures and subverted the process by presenting ways to resist. People disliked being forced to incriminate themselves and began to demand a fair trial; to know the accusations against them and the names of their accusers. They also wanted the right to remain silent when asked questions even when accused of murder.

Unfortunately, Foxe's book and his values of religious freedom and freedom of speech didn't stop Thomas Rowland and Anthony Arrowsmith from being pressed.

August 7th, 1578

Above: Palace Green, near Durham Cathedral.

Thomas Rowland was pressed to death on Palace Green, Durham on August 7th, 1578 and buried at St. Nicholas' Church.

Right: St. Nicholas' Church, Durham Market Place. There has been a church on this site since the early 12th century. The present church was built in 1858.

August 26th, 1597

Anthony Arrowsmith was accused of murder, but said nothing at his trial. He was pressed to death in Durham Market Place.

Today the north is renowned for being a friendly place to visit, but in the past, we do not appear to have taken kindly to strangers who looked different to us.

No Hanging About

August 8th, 1592

Listed in the register of St. Nicholas parish in the city of Durham is the following: *'Simson, Arrington, Fetherstone, Fenwicke, and Lanckaster, "were hanged for being Egyptians."'* (*Sykes, Vol. 1, p.81*)

'Egyptians' appears to be a term applied to those who were dark skinned or more probably Romany gypsies. It obviously didn't pay to look different and if you were convicted of a serious crime, other than treachery, there were always people ready to hang you.

1602

Andrew Tate was hanged on the high road where the road forked for Auckland and Ferryhill. He was convicted of robbery and murder of a number of people at Burnhall, near Sunderland Bridge, County Durham.

If you counterfeited coins and were involved in *'coining'*, making a coin from base metal, then this was done with the intention of debasing coinage, thus creating a financial loss for individuals or the country on a grand scale. But does someone convicted of *'coining'* deserve the ultimate penalty?

1564

A man called Partrage was caught and executed for coining money in the *'great innes of Pilgrim Street'*. (*Sykes, Vol 1, p.76*)

Horse stealing was rife in the north, but did this crime also deserve capital punishment?

August 18th, 1618

Thomas Wright was convicted of horse stealing. He was executed at Dryburn, near Durham and buried at St. Oswald's Church, Durham.

One capital crime, if you were a soldier, was *'denying the king's pay'*. If there was more than one who refused to fight, a council of war had a novel way of setting an example to others.

May, 1640 – Death by Lots

'...two sogers (soldiers), for denying the king's pay, was, by council of war, appointed to be shot att, and a pare of gallos (gallows) set up before Thos. Malaber's dore (door), in the Byg Market. They cust (cast) lotes (lots) which should dy (die) and the lotes did fall one Mr. Anthone Vicaars: and he was set against the wall and shott att by 6 light horsemen, and was buried in the churchyard the same day, May 16th ...'
(*St. Andrew's Church, Newcastle*)

A later view of the Bigg Market, Newcastle.

Murders

Of course there have been murders since man could wield a club. Sometimes the crime wasn't recorded, but the punishment and place of burial were.

December 16th, 1495 – The Bells! The Bells!

In 1481 a Gateshead labourer, John Bonar, knifed and killed Alexander Stevenson near Doteland Park, Hexhamshire.

Fourteen years later, Bonar frantically knocked the huge metal ring on the door to Durham Cathedral and claimed sanctuary.

The abbey church and churchyard was a safe haven for anyone who had committed a serious offence or escaped from prison. Two men were always in two rooms above the North Door listening for the sound of the knocker at night. When they allowed Bonar to enter, they would have run to strike the Galilee bell so that everyone was aware someone had asked for a place of safety.

Entrance to Durham Cathedral.

A facsimile of the Sanctuary Knocker is on the northern door of Durham Cathedral. The 12th century original is in the Cathedral Treasures Exhibit inside.

Once the prior was informed, Bonar would have been dressed in a, *'gown of black cloth'* with St. Cuthbert's yellow cross on the left shoulder. He'd have stayed within the church on a specially made grate near the south door of the gallery and been given, *'meat, drink and bedding, and other necessaries, at the expense of the house, for 37 days'* until he obtained his, *'Prince's pardon'* or, *'the prior and convent'* got him away from the diocese. Durham Cathedral was indeed a sanctuary for those who'd broken the law. (*Sykes, Vol. 1, p.65*)

The nobility sometimes broke the law too and because they were close to royalty their foul deeds were remembered. This was so in the case of the murderer of David Rizzio.

March 9th, 1566 – Rizzio Riddle

When David Riccio di Pancalieri in Piemonte was born in Turin, Italy around 1533, his family would not have envisaged his untimely end in a foreign country. He was also known as David Riccio, Rizzo or more famously as Rizzio and was forever to have his name linked to Mary Queen of Scots.

Several of Rizzio's Scottish murderers: Lord Patrick Ruthven; Lord James Douglas, 4th Earl of Morton; Partick Lindsay, 6th Earl of Lindsay of the Byres and possibly William Maitland fled to Newcastle. These men, under suspicion of Rizzio's murder, were in England under Elizabeth I's protection. Such political interference could only create more problems for Mary Queen of Scots and points to English involvement in Rizzio's death.

Rizzio was a young musician and valet who arrived in the Scottish court with the Ambassador of the Duke of Savoy. Mary Queen of Scots made Rizzio her confidential secretary in place of her Guise retainer, Augustine Raulet, and this overt show of favour made him a target for murder.

Mary at 15 years of age had first been married to 13 year old Francois II of France. He reigned for a year and died. Mary returned to a Scottish court which swirled with political and religious intrigue. Nobles vied for power; England and Scotland had a difficult relationship and there were tensions between Catholics and Calvinist Protestants.

As a Catholic, Mary tolerated Protestants; allied herself with her illegitimate half-brother, James Stewart, Earl of Moray and refused to sign the Treaty of Edinburgh in 1560, despite her own secretaries' approval. The treaty would have loosened the links between Scotland and France and acknowledged Elizabeth I as Queen of England. Rejecting Elizabeth I's favourite, Robert Dudley, Earl of Leicester as a potential husband, Mary married her 19 year old cousin, Henry Stuart, Lord Darnley, on July 5th, 1565.

In March 1565, Darnley became embroiled in a plot against Mary with lords she was going to have tried for treason. They agreed Darnley would become king and the seemingly innocent Rizzio would be the scapegoat. He would be blamed for orchestrating a movement towards Catholicism and misleading Darnley. The plotters also convinced Darnley, that Rizzio had cuckolded him. There may also have been the suggestion that Mary's baby, later to be James VI of Scotland and James I of England, was not his. If Mary miscarried and died, the throne could be Darnley's.

The Scottish Lords Lindsay, Maitland and Ruthven, with the Earl of Morton murdered Rizzio when he was having supper with Mary and some friends at Holyrood Palace, Edinburgh on March 9th, 1566. Rizzio was hauled out of the room and stabbed to death.

Ruthven, a Protestant reformer, had encouraged the match between Mary and Darnley and got out of his sick bed to lead the murder of Rizzio. On returning to Scotland he led a conspiracy which culminated in the *'Raid of Ruthven'* in 1582 when the young James VI was abducted and held for a year. Ruthven took

Holyrood Palace, Edinburgh.

over the reins of government, was pardoned by James VI, but all his honours were forfeited and he was executed in May, 1584.

The Earl of Morton, had a particularly nasty end. He and his son allegedly stayed in the borders and Alnwick until they were granted a pardon and returned to Scotland. Morton became one of the most powerful men in Scotland and the last of four regents to young James VI. However, those who are in power often make enemies and Morton appeared to have been avaricious, ambitious and lacked principles. When Captain James Stuart, son of Lord Ochiltree and brother-in-law of John Knox, daringly accused Morton, of conspiring in Darnley's murder, Morton's days were numbered.

Morton, was tried, convicted and beheaded in Edinburgh in June, 1581, ironically, by *'The Maiden'* a guillotine he'd purchased in Halifax, England. His head was stuck on top of the public gaol, whilst an old cloak covered his body till sunset. He was buried, apparently friendless, amongst criminals and was universally condemned by the Scots.

Lindsay, one of the leaders of the Reformation in Scotland, was probably one of the most violent. He fought in battles for and against Mary, and was brother-in-law and ally to Lord Moray. Lindsay and Ruthven having defeated Mary at the Battle of Carberry

Hill in 1567, took her via Edinburgh to Lindsay's castle at Lochleven. Given the ultimatum, abdicate or die, Mary signed the Deed of Abdication in favour of her son. When Moray was murdered in 1570, Lindsay supported James VI.

Lindsay became Joint Lord Lieutenant and Justice in 1572; Lord Provost of Edinburgh in 1573 and Sherriff of Fife of the Bailliary of St. Andrews in 1574 and was one of the conspirators in the '*Raid of Ruthven*'. He then fled to England. In 1578 he was one of those behind Morton's drive to power. Lindsay died, apparently in his bed in 1589.

Maitland was secretary to Mary and a reformer. He was an ally of Moray and an ambassador in Elizabeth I's court. After Mary abdicated and fled to England, he acted on her behalf in the new government. He wanted Mary to be Elizabeth I's successor. In 1573 he was one of the men who held Edinburgh Castle for Mary.

The Regent requested aid from Elizabeth I and the castle fell. Maitland, already ill, was taken to Leith Prison where he either died from disease or committed suicide in 1573.

The Edinburgh Castle we see today was built in the 12th century.

Darnley was murdered on February 10th, 1567, probably with Mary's knowledge and her third husband, James Hepburn 4th Earl of Bothwell, who allegedly raped her to force her into the marriage, was implicated in the plot. After a sham trial, Bothwell was acquitted. As a point of interest, he died raving mad after being incarcerated in a cell in the Danish fortress of Dragsholm. Apparently his mummified remains can still be viewed in the church of Faareveile, near Dragsholm.

Even Mary came to an untimely end. Elizabeth I signed her death warrant and Mary was executed on February 8th, 1587 at Fotheringhay Castle in Northamptonshire, only a mound and token stone remain.

Fotheringhay Castle, Northamptonshire, sits by the River Nene. The castle, built in the 12th century, fell into disrepair after Mary Queen of Scots' execution and locals helped themselves to the stone. Only a small amount of masonry remains.

It's surprising that the nobility didn't pay someone else to kill Rizzio. However, as modern crime statistics less than comfortingly reveal, it's usually a neighbour, friend or relative that is most likely to murder you! A pity John and Margaret Brass, didn't have these statistics to hand.

January 25th, 1684 – Murder at Ferryhill

John and Margaret Brass, from Ferryhill, County Durham went out on Christmas visits leaving their servant, Andrew Mills, who was 18 or 19, their son who was 18 and two daughters 11 and 20 at home. The 20 year old was looking forward to her wedding.

Mills was described as being a, '*quiet, unoffending lad*' and of, '*somewhat deranged or deficient intellect.*' According to his confession, he acted on, '*an immediate suggestion of the devil*' when he probably murdered the son first. The eldest girl struggled with him for some time and used her arm as a bolt on a door to protect the sleeping youngest. Mills finally broke her arm and murdered her. He then entered the room and used one blow of an axe on the sleeping, younger girl. On leaving the house he heard a voice or felt something saying, '*Kill all! Kill all!*' He returned, dragged the youngest girl from under the bed and completed what he'd started. Having made no attempt to escape, he was found amongst his bleeding victims.

On August 15th, 1684, Mills was tried and executed to the north of Ferryhill, on the common beside the road where he'd committed the murder. The gibbet was named Andrew Mill's stob. An altar tomb was erected in Merrington churchyard to commemorate the tragedy. (*Sykes, Vol. 1, p.118*)

Ferryhill, County Durham – showing the old A1.

Was the murder at Maiden's Bower in the 18th century committed by a friend, stranger or stalker?

Murder at Maiden's Bower

In 1727 a Northallerton grocer, William Stephenson, threw pregnant Mary Farding into the sea, near the Maiden's Bower, Hartlepool. He was found guilty of her murder and hanged at Durham.

What did I write about your nearest and dearest being most likely to murder you?

Beehive Inn, Fishburn, near Sedgefield, County Durham.

Mad Moment

On April 17th, 1741 whilst a farmer named Charlton from Fishburn, Durham was rescuing his cow from a ditch, his wife used a cleaver to kill their 14 year old son, two younger children and herself. The coroner's verdict was lunacy. Had she survived, farmer Charlton's wife would probably have been confined in degrading conditions in either a prison or a private madhouse. Treatment was harsh, mechanical restraint was used and the accommodation was meagre. These madhouses had existed in Britain for a number of centuries; they held the rich and poor (if the fees were paid by their Parish). Clergymen, doctors and laymen ran these institutions for a profit and handled from 1-100 patients.

You didn't have to be mentally ill to kill someone, sometimes alcohol played a part.

August 27th, 1751 – Surgeon killed in Scuffle

Henry Douglas was six feet tall when he joined the navy as a surgeon in 1710. He left in 1712 to join the regiment of foot as a surgeon-major. When he married, he '*quitted it for a home practice, which he discharged with success and approbation, until another war called him back to the fleet.*' After '*the peace*' he settled in Newcastle on half pay.

At between 10 and 11pm, sixty year old, Douglas, described as, '*a man of intrepid courage, good sense, real friendship, and genteel address*' quarrelled with sailor, Edward Holliday, in David Shield's inn, Newcastle. Douglas was killed in the '*scuffle*'. Holliday was tried at the assizes and acquitted. (*Sykes, Vol. 1, p.200*)

Women convicted of murder were usually punished more harshly than men. '*Mustard Bet*' was such a woman.

The Execution of 'Mustard Bet'

Elizabeth Herring, alias '*Mustard Bet*' was born in Newcastle. Whilst aboard the sloop-of-war, *The Peggy* she and her husband, who'd been impressed, were shipwrecked on December 18th, 1770.

She was tried and convicted of murdering him at the Old Bailey. Her punishment was to be drawn on a hurdle from Newgate to Tyburn, tied to a stake, strangled and then burnt.

To be executed like '*Mustard Bet*' was bad enough, but the bodies of John Winship and Thomas Nicholson weren't left in peace even when they were dead.

July 25th, 1785

John Winship, a farmer from Monkwearmouth gave his maidservant certain drugs to induce an abortion. He was convicted of poisoning her and executed at Durham. His body was then given to the surgeons '*for dissection.*' Mr. Wilkinson from Sunderland gave a lecture to numerous '*gentlemen of the faculty on the contents of cranium, thorax, and abdomen.*'
(*Sykes, Vol. 1, p.336*)

August 8th, 1795
Purvis Murder

Thomas Nicholson and a group of pitmen assaulted Thomas Purvis at the races in Newcastle. After they'd beaten Purvis, Nicholson returned and jumped on him. When convicted, Nicholson accepted that the sentence was just, but said he hadn't meant to murder Purvis. Nicholson was executed on the Town Moor, Newcastle and his body was taken to the Surgeon's Hall for dissection.

We always feel sorry for the victims of murders, but spare a thought for the unfortunate porters who worked at post coach offices in 18th century Newcastle. They certainly didn't welcome what they received several times in the post.

St. Peter's Church, Monkwearmouth, Sunderland.

With the introduction of the post coach, passengers, news and mail travelled faster than ever before. Mail could be letters, packets, parcels and boxes. Both the Turk's Head and the Turf Hotel in Newcastle received mail, but in the early 19th century several trunks/boxes were delivered to the Turf Hotel. Their horrific contents must have shaken those who dealt with them.

Body Snatchers
September 16th, 1825

Someone, dressed as a porter, deposited a travelling trunk at the Turf Hotel coach-office, Collingwood Street, Newcastle to be forwarded to Edinburgh the next day. It was addressed to James Syme, Esq., 6, Forth Street, Edinburgh.

Unfortunately the trunk was left amongst packages which were meant for the coach going south and no coaches were going north on Sunday. So it wasn't till Monday that someone detected a sickening smell and liquid seeping from the box.

Magistrates ordered that the box be opened. Inside was a female corpse! She was thought to be about nineteen, with light eyes, fair hair and complexion. There were no marks of violence on the body. After a coroner's inquest the body was interred.

The post coach first appeared in 1784. It provided a new form of transport; ensured the swift delivery of newspapers to the provinces and journey times were cut by two thirds. Left: Outside the Kenton Post Office is the Royal Mail coach that made the journey from Newcastle to Kirkwhelpington, Northumberland. In 1905 this coach was robbed on the highway near Kenton.

January 6th, 1826

It was night when the Leeds Telegraph coach dropped off a box in Newcastle. It was addressed to Mr. Simpson, 61, Princes Street, Edinburgh and weighed approximately 16 stone. Suspicions were aroused as several similar boxes had already passed through Newcastle. When the police opened the box they found, to their horror, a male corpse! He was over six foot tall, aged between 40-50 years, with black hair and Roman nose. He'd only recently died.

The next morning the coroner stated: '*no marks of violence appear on the body, but by what means he came to his death, no evidence doth appear.*' The body was then interred. (*Sykes, Vol. 2, p.190*)

January 15th, 1826

The gruesome discovery was made of a man's corpse in a common deal box in the Turf Hotel coach-office, Collingwood Street. It had arrived from beyond York bound for Edinburgh. The body was buried at Ballast Hills.

January 26th, 1826

Yet another box arrived from the south at the Turf Hotel coach-office and contained the body of a little, elderly woman. She was also buried at Ballast Hills.

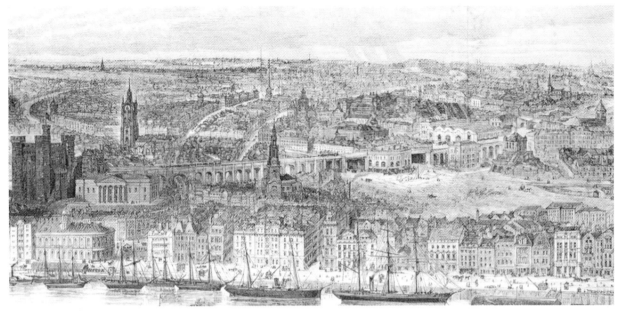

A sketch of Newcastle from the 1800s.

November 11th, 1828

Two boxes arrived in the coach-office of the Turf Hotel, Newcastle. The first was carried on the York Highflyer coach on the 8th and the other was brought to the office by a man. Both parcels were bound for different addresses in Edinburgh. Suspicions were aroused and the first parcel was sent back to York, but the coach proprietor returned it to Newcastle. The police were contacted and two dead females were found.

Inquests were held the following day and the coroner's verdict was that there were no signs of violence on the bodies. They were buried in St. John's churchyard. The man who took the second box to the coach-office was tried and acquitted.

In the 19th century a profit could be made from corpses and there appears to have been *'extensive traffic'* between resurrectionists in England and anatomy lecturers in Edinburgh as only the bodies of convicted felons who had been hanged were allowed to be dissected.

What is tantalising is the thought, if the accounts above are accurate, that the Turf Hotel in Newcastle was a link in the chain to the infamous body snatchers, Burke and Hare, or people of their ilk, in Edinburgh.

Between 1827-1828 Dr. Robert Knox, a Scottish surgeon, anatomist and zoologist purchased 17 'cadavers' (one died of natural causes the others by suffocation) from Irishmen Burke and Hare. Knox was in charge of Barclay's anatomy school in Surgeon's Square. His unusual teaching style and the fact he could guarantee human corpses to dissect, made him popular with medical students. His role in the Burke and Hare affair is portrayed in a rhyme of the time;

> *'Up the Close and doun the stair;*
> *But and ben wi' Burke and Hare:*
> *Burke's the butcher, Hare's the thief,*
> *And Knox the boy who stole the beef.'*

Burke, his partner Helen and Hare were put on trial on Christmas Eve, 1828. Hare turned King's Evidence and was freed. Burke was convicted and hanged on January 28th, 1829; Helen was given the judgement of not proven; and Knox, though acquitted for his part in the crimes, left Edinburgh for London and became a pathologist at the Royal Marsden Hospital, lectured, wrote and had a general practice.

Right: The Surgeons' Hall, Edinburgh.

Unexpected Deaths

Murder is an appalling crime, but death can, of course, come in many different ways.

January 16th, 1776 – Twelve Snuffed out by Snow

'A heavy fall of snow commenced at Newcastle continued almost without intermission all that night and the next day. The frost was almost uncommonly; and six men and six women perished in the neighbourhood of the town.' (*Mackenzie, 1827*)

Northumberland in winter.

June 28th, 1786 – Beastly Boar

A boar owned by Graham Clarke, Esq. escaped and servant Joseph Smith was sent to capture it. He cornered the beast in a narrow lane between the Town Wall and High Friar Street, Newcastle. Smith threw stones at the boar to drive it back home. Infuriated, the animal savaged Smith's thigh, turned on others so they had to jump over a wall and returned to attack his victim again. Smith died minutes later. The boar was shot.

Whilst some were killed by rampaging animals in narrow streets, others died because of their adventurous spirit.

September 19th, 1786 – Up, Up and ...!

Vincenzo Lunardi was famous for making the first manned hydrogen balloon ascent in Great Britain. He was born on January 11th, 1759, in Lucca, Italy. Through his interest in flying hydrogen balloons, he was to find fame in London and his downfall (pardon the pun) in Newcastle.

On November 21st, 1783, Jean-Francoise Pilatre de Rozier and Francois Laurent d'Arlandes using a Montgolfier Brothers' hot air balloon, were the first to fly with no tether. The flight lasted 25 minutes, they reached an altitude of 3,000ft and flew for two miles. Physicist, Jacques Charles, and Nicolas Roberts made an ascent with no tether less than two weeks later. The daring Frenchmen's flying exploits captured the imagination of France.

One year later, James Tytler, the *'Flying Scot'* impressed Scotland when he built the Grand Edinburgh Fire Balloon and made the first hot air flight above British soil. Sadly, English attempts at manned balloon flights had resulted in failure and the country remained sceptical about flying.

Described as a dandy, Lunardi came to London in the employment of the Neapolitan Ambassador. He was young and handsome and perhaps spurred on by the fashionable talk about French aeronauts. Anyway, Lunardi teamed up with George Biggin, a patron of the

Vincenzo Lunardi.

arts, to learn more about aeronautics. Lunardi was to prove himself an entrepreneur, brave and a showman.

He was an entrepreneur because his was to be the first manned, public flight in a hydrogen balloon in Great Britain. Brave because his balloon was composed of silk which he filled with hydrogen gas, a known and highly volatile substance created by the heady mix of sulphuric acid, water and iron filings in huge vats on his take off sites. He was a showman because his flights attracted enormous crowds and he achieved the fame he appeared to seek.

Lunardi's training ground was north of London at Moorfields. His maiden flight took place on September 15th, 1784 when he took off in his red and blue striped hydrogen balloon from the ground of the Honourable Artillery Company.

George Biggin was apparently supposed to be aboard, but Lunardi had problems inflating the balloon, the crowd became restless and he set off without the correct amount of hydrogen. He carried oars in the belief that they would act as they did in a boat. One oar broke as the balloon floated upwards. His travelling companions were a cat, a dog and a pigeon. Crowds of 100,000-150,000, the Prince of Wales and numerous statesmen, tipped their hats as he ascended and according to one account the pigeon escaped early on in the flight.

Staying at altitudes of 1,000ft, Lunardi experienced temperatures as low as minus 16 degrees C. He landed temporarily in a cornfield at Welham Green near the parish of North Mimms at 3.30pm. It's now called Balloon Corner and is 13 miles from London. There are conflicting reports about how many animals he released here, but he also got rid of the last of his ballast. A commemorative stone at Balloon Corner records the momentous flight.

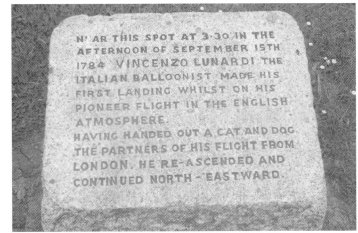

The commemorative stone at Balloon Corner stands on a grass triangle in the middle of a housing estate.

Lunardi took off again, and flew at a higher altitude. Thirty to forty minutes later he landed more than 20 miles away in a field at Colliers End, near Ware in Hertfordshire. According to accounts, the local farmers were too frightened to grab the ropes and only did so when local girl, Elizabeth Brett, seized one. Accounts also say that balloonists were irresistible to the ladies. Near a house called Long Mead there's a monument in a field with these word inscribed on it:

'Let posterity know, and knowing be astonished, that on the fifteenth day of September, 1784, Vincent Lunardi of Lucca, in Tuscany, the first aerial traveller in Britain, mounting from the Artillery Ground in London, and traversing the regions of the air for two hours and fifteen minutes, in this spot revisited the earth. On this rude monument for ages be recorded this wondrous enterprise successfully achieved by the powers of chemistry and the fortitude of man, this improvement in science which the great author of all knowledge, patronizing by his Providence the inventions of mankind hath graciously permitted, to their benefit and his own eternal glory.'

Apparently several men on horseback, who'd followed Lunardi's flight from London, bought him a celebratory drink in the Bull Inn at Ware, Hertfordshire.

Calling himself, the *'First Aerial Traveller in England'*, Lunardi became the toast of London. The world of English fashion was so inspired that a Lunardi bonnet, which was balloon shaped and 2ft high, was created; skirts were designed bearing Lunardi motifs and Lunardi petticoats and garters became fashionable. One wag wrote a poem commenting on women wearing fashionable Lunardi garters:

'Below her knee, or round her thigh
His dear enchanting name did tie;
And shew'd the bold advent'rer more
Of Heaven then e'er he saw before.'

Lauded as a hero, Lunardi was presented to George III and made several more flights in balloons decorated with the union flag. He took Mrs. Letitia Sage, an actress on her first flight, making her the first British female to fly in a balloon and made several long distance flights across Scotland in '*The Grand Air Balloon*' made of 1,500ft of green, pink and yellow silk. Two of these attempts proved manned hydrogen balloon flights a dangerous activity.

A dissenting preacher, Lothian Tam, in his desperate endeavours to see Lunardi's second ascent, became entangled in the balloon's ropes. He was lifted 20ft in to the air! Fortunately, though he fell, he wasn't injured.

When Lunardi ascended from Heriot's Hospital in Edinburgh, strong winds forced him to ditch into the sea and he was picked up by a fishing boat and landed at North Berwick.

Perhaps these were warnings. If so, Lunardi appeared to ignore them when he arrived in Newcastle.

Whilst Mr. Lunardi was preparing his balloon to ascend above Newcastle, a dreadful accident occurred. Lunardi pulled a plug from a funnel causing a noise when gas was released. This caused consternation amongst those who were holding the ropes and keeping the balloon on the ground.

Some men released the ropes on one side of the balloon tearing its neck where it was connected to the barrel. Despite Lunardi's strenuous attempts to keep the balloon on the ground, more ropes were released and the balloon flew up into the air.

Ralph Heron, the 22 year old son of the Under-Sheriff of Northumberland had coiled a rope, attached to the top of his balloon, round his arm. He did not or could not release it and was hoisted upward at great speed. His weight caused the balloon to rotate and the top and netting were torn off. Heron plummeted to the ground and landed in a garden with the cries and groans of thousands of spectators ringing in his ears.

Apparently there were no outward signs of injury, but he complained of pain in his back

Lunardi's balloon taking off from the Artillery Ground, London, September 15th, 1784.

and intestines. He was able to speak to surgeons and his parents, but died ninety minutes later.

Probably to damp down the public outcry, Lunardi printed a handbill:

'*Mr. Lunardi is deeply afflicted for the melancholy accident that attended his endeavours to gratify the curiosity of the public with the ascension of his balloon; and it is only to be consoled by the reflection of its having been occasioned by circumstances which it was not in his power to prevent. It remains for him to yield to his own wish to fulfil the expectation of the town, to the feelings of a parent, wounded by the loss of a most amiable son; and to forbear a repetition in this town, which, without fault on his part, has been fatal to the peace of a respectable family. The unvaried success of his former exhibitions, though the rememberance of it now serves but to embitter his grief, will, he hopes, rescue him, in the eyes of a just and generous people, from any imputation injurious to his honour. – King's Arms, Newcastle, Wednesday, September 20th, 1786.*' (Sykes, Vol.1, p.341)

Lunardi bewailed Heron's death. Then said he'd warned everything would be safe as long as no one let go of a rope.

The *Newcastle Chronicle* declared Lunardi blameless and sniped at London newspapers with their suggestions that provincials had run him off. Lunardi in fact left Great Britain never to return, but he continued his balloon ascents in Italy, Portugal and Spain. He died in Portugal, unmarried and at 47 years of age on July 31st, 1806.

Section Two – Disasters

Disasters in coal mines; freak weather conditions; fires; plague and pestilence and 'runs' on banks, the North East has seen them all.

The Wingate Grange Lodge Banner leads the funerals at Wingate, County Durham, after twenty-four men were killed following an explosion in 1906.

King Coal

A Report by Jon Roby Leifchild on 'The Employment of Children and Young Persons in the Collieries, Lead Mines and Iron Works of Northumberland and the North of Durham; and on the Condition, Treatment, and Education of such Children and Young

Jarrow Colliery (also known as Temple Main Colliery) – a sketch by Thomas Hair.

Persons' was presented to Parliament in 1842. According to the Report's findings there were 7,261 adults; 1,932 young persons and 1,349 children employed in Tyne collieries (a few small collieries were omitted) and it gave some insight into the appalling working conditions these people had to endure in the pits at this time. However, the real facts may have been hidden by workers frightened of losing their employment.

In the 1840s Jarrow Colliery was given the name '*the slaughterhouse*' because of its high death rate. Gas in the Bensham seam caused numerous explosions. In the early 19th century there were seven major explosions, the worst was in 1830 killing 42 miners, and in 1845 leaving 39 dead. It's not surprising its workers were asked to contribute to the 1842 report.

No. 335 Mr. Jobling, the viewer (an early mine engineer) at Jarrow Colliery, appeared to have only a positive view of work conditions at the pit. He told the commissioning officers that pit workers were mostly better off than other labourers in terms of pay, food and health.

The young rolley drivers below were aged between 12-14 years of age, worked a shift in the colliery from 3am to 3pm, earned 1s 3d per day and tell us of the accidents they had.

No. 346 David Fairgeave said he fell down and broke his leg when the rollies went over him. He was off work for 3 months and was lame at present.
No. 347 William Robson claimed he fell off the limmers of the rolley and the wheels ran over him and hurt his left arm. He was off work for 24 days.

The medical attendant at the colliery, W. Brown Esq., appeared to have had a low opinion of pitmen, describing them as self-willed and ignorant. He also stated in writing that their work at the pit had no effect on their physical condition, except perhaps skin diseases.

At Monkwearmouth, Washington and Belmont Collieries, No. 367 Mr. George Elliot, the head viewer, reported that parents have put him under a lot of pressure to hire boys from 6 years of age and he knew of 5 year old boys working in the pit.

In 1842 there were serious problems with the hours the boys were expected to work in a day; the age of pit workers and their poor

The cramped working conditions undeground at a Durham Colliery in 1905.

opportunities for education. All combined to ensure generations of families stayed impoverished and in the pit. How did this come about? For an answer we need to look at the origins of coal mining in the north and the horror that followed.

The First Coal Dug in the North

Records indicate that it was in Durham in the 12th century that monks first dug for coal. The first coal dug in Newcastle came from Castle Field and the Forth and in 1239 a charter was granted by King Henry III. A stranger took his life into his hands if he rode into Newcastle in 1256, as there were so many deserted pits nearby.

The name '*pitman*' first appeared in the early 13th century, when coal was exhausted above the ground and men began to dig pits and go underground.

The first mention of the term '*colliery*' appears to have been used in 1330. There were collieries at Heygrove in the East and West-Fields and near Gallow-flat at 'Elstewicke' (Elswick, near Newcastle) owned by the prior of Tynemouth. He let out Hygrove for £5 and the pit in the East-field for 5 marks a year.

In 1357 the men of Newcastle were granted licenses from King Edward III to dig for coal in Castle Field and Castle Moor. It was also decreed that coals dug in Gateshead had to be ferried across the Tyne to Newcastle as long as they paid the port duty. Then the coal could be taken anywhere in England and Calais. This was the first year coal was exported from Newcastle to London, but what was the cost in human lives?

The records reveal the first deaths in coal mines were in 1329 at Thrislington and Whickham. Perhaps the roof of the mine caved in or the props gave way. The records don't tell us.

HOW ARE YOU OFF FOR COALS?

A smiling pitman on an advert for domestic coal.

23

In the 16th century, flooding in the deeper mines in Tyneside became problematic. 'Gin-gans' or horse-drawn engines were used in 1580 to pump out the water.

But sometimes nature wouldn't be harnessed as in August, 1648 when a terrible storm flooded the best collieries on the River Wear. And when over a decade later in May, 1658, water broke into a Galla-Flatt (near Elswick) coal pit from an old waste and James Archer and his son Stephen drowned. Their bodies were found 36 years and 11 months later and buried at St. Andrew's Church, Newcastle on April 24th, 1695.

Flooding didn't stop coal mining. In 1280 Newcastle had doubled its worth on the back of the coal trade and by the 16th century £10,000 was raised in a tax on coal. In the 17th century, after the Fire of London, a coal tax helped to rebuild St. Paul's Cathedral as well as fifty churches in the capital city.

However, water wasn't the only hazard underground. The register at St. Mary's Church, Newcastle, records that Richard Backus was, 'burnt in a pit' in 1618. Fire also spelt disaster at Benwell in the 18th century.

St. Andrew's Church, Newgate Street, begun in the 12th century.

Benwell Fire Spreads to Fenham

In the early 1700s a fire took hold in a coal mine near Benwell, Newcastle which burnt for thirty years. It spread to Fenham and burst out like a volcano spurting forth sulphur and sal ammoniac (a white salt used in dry cells). A candle flame appears to have been the cause.

It wasn't a candle flame that started the next blaze during a period of intense cold at Tanfield Colliery on January 12th, 1740.

Inferno at Tanfield Colliery

A fire was lit. At 2 am boys were instructed to put it out after the workmen left, but were apparently careless. Straw caught alight and the fire spread to two oil casks and the coal. The flames fanned by fresh air from nearby pits became a raging inferno and huge, hot cinders were flung high into the air and landed a considerable distance away. The blaze increased to such an extent, that several who attempted to put it out almost died. The pit was closed up and the fire extinguished.

Flood and fire were serious threats to life underground, but there was also 'foul air' or gas. The presence of firedamp or methane gas could lead to explosions; after damp or carbon monoxide gas; blackdamp or chokedamp (a low level of oxygen and high level of carbon dioxide) could occur after an explosion; stinkdamp or hydrogen sulphide gas and stythe gas could also kill you. So not only did miners face the possibility of being blown up, but if they survived the blast they could then be asphyxiated.

Memorial cards such as this were often produced after mining disasters. This one is in memory of fourteen pitmen killed following an explosion at Glebe Colliery, Washington, in 1908.

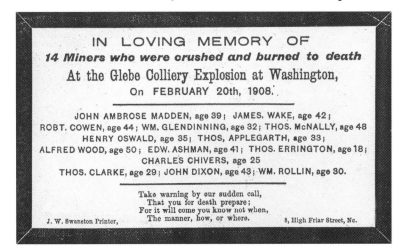

IN LOVING MEMORY OF
14 Miners who were crushed and burned to death
At the Glebe Colliery Explosion at Washington,
On FEBRUARY 20th, 1908.

JOHN AMBROSE MADDEN, age 39; JAMES. WAKE, age 42;
ROBT. COWEN, age 44; WM. GLENDINNING, age 32; THOS. McNALLY, age 48
HENRY OSWALD, age 35; THOS. APPLEGARTH, age 33;
ALFRED WOOD, age 50; EDW. ASHMAN, age 41; THOS. ERRINGTON, age 18;
CHARLES CHIVERS, age 25
THOS. CLARKE, age 29; JOHN DIXON, age 43; WM. ROLLIN, age 30.

Take warning by our sudden call,
That you for death prepare;
For it will come you know not when,
The manner, how, or where.

J. W. Swanston Printer,   8, High Friar Street, Ne.

Methane gas, once ignited, could explode with horrendous consequences as it did in the 18th century at the North Biddick, Walker, South Biddick and Chatershaugh Collieries.

Explosion at North Biddick Colliery

The colliery, on the River Wear experienced an explosion at 5am on January 28th, 1743. It was caused by workmen digging into a drift linked to an old waste which filled with water and the foul air exploded. Ten men and five boys lost their lives and others died later from their injuries.

Twenty-three years later, on March 18th, 1766, ten men were killed when there was an explosion at Walker Colliery. The following month there was an explosion in South Biddick Colliery on April 16th, 1766 and several lives were lost.

North Biddick Colliery alongside the banks of the Wear.

Gas!

It was 2am on August 11th, 1765 when gas ignited at one of the pits at Chatershaugh Colliery on the River Wear. Four men died when they were torn apart in the blast. The explosion was like cannon fire and could be heard two miles away. A corfe of coals, lying 80 fathoms down the shaft was also thrown up into the sky and coal dust and rubbish were scattered on the ground. The coal dust could also have ignited, triggered by the initial methane gas explosion. Fortunately, not all of the miners were underground.

Conditions have always been extremely dangerous in mines, but because many coalowners put profit before the safety of their work force; insisted miners signed an annual contract called a Bond, which legally ensured they worked for a year for the pit owner; paid poor wages commonly in the form of a *'Tommy check'* which could only be redeemed in the pit owner's Tommy-shop; rented cottages to miners that whole families could be forced from and so on, relationships between some coalowners and miners broke down in the 18th and 19th centuries.

Strike!

In 1765 there were miners' strikes in Durham and Northumberland. Pitmen were bound either at the end of August or the beginning of September, 1764. However, they were not freed from their bond till the November 11th, 1765, more than three months longer than they should have been. Instead of being tied by the bond to work 11 months and 25 days, they were tied for 14 months. The miners demanded that this issue should be resolved and new bonds agreed for the following year.

On September 18th the coal mine and one of the pits at Pelton Common

Miners on strike at Waldridge, County Durham.

Colliery in County Durham, owned by Mrs. Jennison and partners, were set on fire. The owners offered £100 reward for the discovery of the arsonist.

Deliberate acts of destruction such as this are perhaps understandable, but indefensible. However, human error, ignorance or greed also presented real problems.

Did the Earth Move For You?

The terrified inhabitants of Long Benton, four miles from Newcastle, fled their homes on November 27th, 1765. They experienced a shock like an earthquake. Their houses shook so much they were expected to immediately fall down. A crack opened and closed along the street; one man's garden and fields sank approximately two feet and parts of Killingworth Moor followed suit.

Apparently Long Benton Colliery had been worked out. Slight wooden pillars replaced those made of coal and couldn't hold up a rock two miles square and 75 fathoms thick which was the depth of the coal pit. This was why the earth moved for the inhabitants of Long Benton.

Long Benton was lucky, no one died. Why replace coal pillars for *'slight'* wooden ones? Was it the colliery owner's greed for coal at any cost that caused the subsidence?

It certainly wasn't an accident unlike that which happened at Lambton Colliery, near Chester-le-Street on August 20th, 1766. One hundred workmen had just left the colliery and three labourers and three masons had just gone down. Their job was to build a partition to secure the coals from taking fire. The masons requested a lamp. There was an

Two stone built houses in Long Benton.

immediate fire and flash which was similar to lightning. The explosion killed men and horses and could be heard for three miles.

All that could be found by rescuers at the mouth and surrounding area of the pit was a collection of heads, arms and legs as well as timber and coals. Everything in the pit like corves, linings, partitions, trap-doors and the engine and apparatus which drew up the coal was blown away.

On the morning of March 17th, 1767 in the colliery at Fatfield, County Durham, which was 80 fathoms deep, thirty-nine people lost their lives in an horrendous explosion.

The *Newcastle Journal* commented on March 27th, 1767 on the, *'deplorable accidents that have lately happened in collieries.'* The paper suggested that the coal owner, *'make provision for the distressed widows and fatherless children ...'*

Strangely the *Journal* states that it was, *'requested to take no particular notice of these things, which, in fact could have very little good tendency, we drop farther from mentioning it ...'*

However, the paper goes on to recommend that provision, like that of Trinity House, for *'distressed seamen and seamen's widows &c ...'* was made for families who experienced colliery disasters. Was it the mine owner who asked the newspaper to ignore the facts? Was the *Journal* at fault for not doing some investigative journalism and perhaps campaigning for improvements in health and safety in the mines?

Stormy Weather

We've all heard of Noah's Ark and the flood in the Bible. We've even lived through flooding on Saturday, September 6th, 2008 when rivers like the Wansbeck broke their banks and damaged 995 properties in Morpeth.

Walking along a riverbank feeding the ducks on a sunny day can be deceptive as rivers and flood plains have always been dangerous places when it's been raining heavily or there is a rapid thaw upstream. Town Planners and developers would do well to learn from history as sometimes the heavens just open and there's not a lot you can do.

The River Wansbeck, looking upstream at Morpeth.

A flood at Walker Gate, Newcastle, in 1913. A century later this same place suffered flash flooding during a torrential downpour on June 28th, 2012. Chaos came to Tyneside that night with numerous roads under feet of water and hundreds of houses flooded.

Floods

The rivers in the north have a long history of flooding, for instance on August 15th, 1339 the River Tyne breached the town walls at the quayside in Newcastle and 167 people were drowned. Perhaps the worst incident of flooding in the north occurred in 1771.

The Great Flood of November 16-17th, 1771
The Tyne

The source of the North Tyne appears to be in a field north west of Kielder. The South Tyne begins at Tyne Head, west of Beaver Rigg in the Pennines south of Alston. Both

The River Tyne, north of Hexham, Northumberland.

rivers combine at Watersmeet near Warren (between Haydon Bridge and Hexham) and become the River Tyne.

Late on Saturday night, November 16th, there was torrential rain in the west, turning streams into rivers which poured into the North and South Tyne and on into the Tyne. Over 62 miles away to the east, at the mouth of the river, a spring tide was expected. Both of these factors combined to create perhaps the worst flood recorded in the area. It was just fortunate the wind blew from the north east, and not the west, or the current of the rivers would have been even faster.

Chollerford Bridge built between 1772-1775 by masons Thomas Forster and William Johnson.

South Tyne near Ridley Hall, Northumberland.

Most of the villages and cottages from Tyne Head in Alston Moor to Shields at the mouth of the river were to suffer severe flooding. The bridges on the South Tyne at Alston, Ridley Hall and Haydon Bridge, and on the North Tyne at Chollerford and the Tyne at Hexham were destroyed. Chollerford had several fords and bridges before a stone bridge was built in 1394, but this was destroyed in the flood of 1771.

The River Allen, as usual, flowed into the South Tyne at Ridley Hall, but the torrent that swept into Allendale's wooden bridge carried it as far as a lane at Newbrough. Apparently the newly arrived bridge looked quite at home.

Haydon Bridge, on the South Tyne, was flooded and men had to wade up to their necks in water, with women and children on their backs, to find safety in the local church.

There have been numerous re-builds of bridges at Hexham. In 1771, Hexham's bridge, with its seven arches, was particularly beautiful. It was designed by William Gott in 1770, but couldn't withstand the flood the following year. The river was recorded to have risen 13ft above its normal level here.

Several houses and estates near Hexham were flooded, though no one lost their life. A man at the West Boat was forced by rising water, to break through the thatch of his house and pull his family to safety on the roof. They were half naked and had to stay there for hours.

Mr. Dunn's corn stacks and estates were inundated by flood water; farms belonging to Mr. Robert Bell and Mr. Harbottle were mostly destroyed as well as Mr. Blackett's estates.

People were said to have stood on the bridge at Corbridge and washed their hands in the water racing beneath it. It was built in 1674 and was the only bridge to survive the floods.

It was felt that a lot of water bypassed it by flowing onto lower ground and that its sturdy foundations meant it was strong enough to withstand the rushing waters.

In Bywell, St. Andrew's, also known as the White Church, had its churchyard wall and churchyard destroyed.

Surging water knocked down Mr. Fenwick's garden fence and swirled over his garden and into his house. Eight feet of water flowed into the first floor rooms. A delay of five minutes, would have meant the loss of four servants and all of Fenwick's valuable stud horses. He managed to save them by getting them into St. Peter's Church, also known as the Black Church. The flood ruined the walls and coffins. Corpses were cast out of the churchyard and the parish accounts were destroyed. The horses, *'saved themselves by holding the tops of the pews.'* (*Sykes, Vol. 1. p.287*)

South Tyne at Haydon Bridge, built in 1773 replacing the earlier bridge lost in 1771.

The present bridge at Hexham was built in 1782. There may have been a 13th century bridge, however, there were ferries. A 1770 bridge designed by William Gott was destroyed in the flood of 1771. Another bridge built down river only lasted from 1781-82.

There have been several bridges at Corbridge. This bridge was built in 1694 and is the last one left standing after the Great Flood of 1771.

Stones taken from a previous Roman Bridge at Corbridge.

Bywell village was completely submerged. Ten houses were washed away, though some of the inhabitants were saved by escaping through their roofs or by grasping ropes, trees and twigs, but six people died.

Apparently the pews displayed the bite marks of the terrified horses for some years after the flood.

Mr. Elliot, Thomas Bewick's father-in-law, was unfortunately visiting Bywell at this time and his mare felt the need to clamber onto the altar in the same church to save its life!

One of the most dramatic stories is that of the Johnson family who lived in the boathouse in Ovingham. Ten people: John Johnson, the boatman, his wife, two children, mother, brother, '*his man*', a maid servant, a labourer, George Simpson and a man from Prudhoe were sleeping in the house that night.

St. Peter's Church, Bywell. Its origins are 12th century. At one point it belonged to the black (Benedictine) monks and was called the Black Church.

The roar of the rising water and debris must have alerted them to the danger they were in. As water spewed into the house, the inhabitants retreated upstairs until they were under the roof, but the water kept rising. Thinking the adjoining stable would remain above the flood water, they broke through the wall and crawled in. Feeling they were safe, they made a place to sit, '*... by putting a deal and ladder betwixt the binding stalks ...*' They stayed there till 1am when to their horror the boathouse was destroyed and the stable was creaking. Climbing onto the roof, three sat on the top of the chimney, but the stable, unable to withstand the rush of water, fell into the flood, taking everyone with it! They were deposited 300 yards away in a wood. Johnson, managed to cling onto a tree with one hand, and his wife with the other for several minutes, but she was eventually wrested from his grasp. He, his brother and a maid servant clambered into the safety of the branches of trees. Out of the ten people who spent the night in the boathouse only two survived as the maid died some time later on dry land. Johnson and his brother remained the sole grieving survivors.

Downstream, three hundred acres at Wylam Colliery were inundated with flood water. The seams contained 1,728,000 hogsheads (a cask containing 63-140 gallons) of water.

At Team, near Swalwell, the swollen River Derwent met the surging Tyne (near what is now the Metro Centre), forcing people to hurriedly escape the rising water through their roofs. One family was saved by grasping onto a boat that had been cast adrift in the raging current and driven into a half submerged house.

In another dwelling, the water was of such a height that an elderly man and his wife were found hanging to their roof timbers, proving that the will to live is a powerful force.

The Lady's Steps (dam head) Swalwell. Nº 2

Children enjoy more peaceful times on the river at Swalwell.

Imagine all this water, ruined bridges, houses, fences, ripped out trees, hedges, fencing, boats, people and livestock rushing down river towards sleeping Newcastle and the coast.

In the early hours of Sunday morning an alarm sounded in Newcastle as the arches under the Tyne Bridge filled with water. The Tyne rose quickly to 12ft above the high water mark of a spring tide and 6ft above the previous flood in 1763. The swollen river surged over the quay sweeping away cargoes such as stacks of timber, merchant goods and tar. Keels and other boats from above and below the bridge were driven out to sea by the current and rapidly rising water or scattered on both banks of the river down to Shields. Three sloops and a brig were thrust into and onto the quay, they wrecked the pavement and were stranded when the flood subsided.

The water then gushed along the Close and Sandhill to its northern corner, to such a depth that a boat was rowed. Cellars, shops, lower floors of houses and warehouses were awash, from the western end of the Close to the Ouseburn. Those living there only just managed to save their lives.

In 1339, one of the first bridges across the Tyne experienced flooding, when the

The old Tyne Bridge.

rush of water swept away a section and apparently 120 people drowned. The ruined bridge was restored in the late 14th-early 15th century and further repairs took place. But in 1771 the Tyne Bridge was crowded with houses and businesses constructed from wood, with a lane in the middle for travellers and a series of arches below.

Within an hour of the flood reaching Newcastle, the Tyne Bridge was unable to withstand the pressure of water and crumbled at its weakest points – the arches. The torrent swept away the north arch next to the toll-house and two others supporting houses near Gateshead.

Seven houses, shops and their inhabitants were completely overwhelmed and disappeared into the fast flowing waters. The buildings that fell into the deluge were inhabited by: Mr. Christopher Byerley, a hardwareman, and his son; the Fiddes family and their maid Ann Tinkler; milliner, Mrs. Haswell; shoemaker, Mr. Hills; cheesemonger, Mr. John James; an apprentice of a Mr. James; glover, Mr. Laybourn; mercer, Mr. Patten and maid; dealer in stuffs and checks, Ann Tinkler; shoemakers, Jon Sharp and Edward Wilson; flax-merchant, Mr. Walton and shoemaker, Mr. Peter Weatherley his wife, two children and a servant girl.

Mr. Christopher Byerley, his son and a Mr. James' apprentice lost their lives at this point. It was not until May 5th, 1772 that Mr. Byerley's body was found amidst the ruins of the bridge.

Mr. Fiddes who lived at the north end of the bridge with his wife, two children and maidservant, Ann Tinkler, escaped across the bridge to safety on the Gateshead side. However, Ann begged Mr. Fiddes to go back with her for her bundle. He reluctantly agreed, but seconds later the arch they were on gave way and they plummeted into the torrent below as his poor wife watched. She never saw her husband again and apparently it wasn't until July, 1772, that Ann Tinkler's body was found.

Perhaps the most heroic tale was that of the Weatherley family and their servant girl. They were woken by the sound of the flood at between 3 and 4am that morning. Mr. Weatherley opened a window and saw the Fiddes family and their servant making their way across the bridge. Thinking little of it, he shut the window when the arch on the north side of his house collapsed! Gathering his family together, he opened the front door so they could run to safety, only to see to his horror the torrent was almost immediately beneath them. Terrified, they made their way to the north end of the bridge, over '... *breaking and tumbling* ...' stone, but were cut off by a fallen arch. Retracing their footsteps they made their way to the southern end of the bridge, but found two fallen arches impeded their escape to Gateshead. The Weatherley family and servant were precariously marooned on a 6ft square portion of the crumbling bridge from 4 to 10am in the middle of the worst flood since records began!

Though inhabitants from both sides of the river were aware of the Weatherleys' plight, no one tried to save them by boat, it was just too dangerous. It was apparent, if they weren't rescued soon, they'd die from exposure or the bridge would collapse with them on it.

Hero, Gateshead bricklayer, George Woodward, decided to risk his life and go to their aid. He utilized several shops which stood on timber on the east side of the bridge and led from Gateshead to where the Weatherleys and the maid servant were huddled. By breaking down the interconnecting

Newcastle's ruined old bridge after the 1771 flood.

walls, Woodward. created a tunnel from one shop to the next and led the terrified Weatherley group and their servant to safety. The cold had exhausted the children.

The torrent rushed on carrying debris with it as it went. Fortunately, Jarrow Slake acted as an overflow for the flood water. In the aftermath, Mr. Patten's house was found whole, near Jarrow Slake, its only inhabitants a cat and dog. The sound wooden structure of the dwelling must have allowed it to float eight miles downstream!

At the river mouth a number of moored ships were driven onto Herd Sands and some were wrecked. One boy was seen clinging to the main-top-mast-head from Sunday to Monday morning. He was eventually saved when conditions allowed a rescue to be mounted. Miraculously, like Moses, a live child in a wooden cradle was also found floating in the sea near Shields!

The Following Days

Four other houses, Mr. Akenhead and Mr. Fawcett owned two each, fell from the ruins of the Tyne Bridge into the river. They were swiftly followed by a host of buildings from near the blue stone on the bridge (the boundary between Newcastle and Gateshead) across to Gateshead.

Just under two weeks later a section of the south end of the weakened Tyne Bridge collapsed taking with it Mr. Laybourn's house and glovers shop. The following day six houses and shops from the blue stone to the south end of the bridge also fell into the river. There was nothing left connecting the Newcastle boundary to Gateshead.

Life on the Tyne continued despite the bridge being in ruins.

Worse was to come. The deaths didn't end with the flood. Apparently, on December 14th, Mrs. Mabane and Mr. Patten's maid, died from the fright, from which they never recovered, suffered on the day of the flood. A woman cradling a child was unfortunately, found drowned at Jarrow Slake. But, Mr. Weatherley, it's interesting to note, died in his own bed in his house at White Hart Yard, the Old Flesh Market, on January 12th, 1826.

At the same time the River Wear was also experiencing flooding.

The Wear

The bridges at Frosterley, Wolsingham and Witton were torn down by the raging water. Durham recorded its highest flood water to date at 8ft 10 inches. The torrent swept away two houses and their contents, standing at the end of Framwellgate Bridge; one of the abbey mills; the Dean and Chapter's Bridge and three of Elvet Bridge's arches. Flooding Durham's lower buildings, the water also wrecked gardens and a number of horses and cattle were drowned in stables and byres.

The River Wear in spate.

Many houses suffered a lot of damage. Mrs. Morgan's house and Mr. Wilkinson's coach-house, in Elvet were pushed down, but the waters were prevented from taking them away, by the houses behind them.

The Wear carried a young woman 700 yards downstream where she was saved by a servant. However, at Cockenford, two of Mr. Carr's servants drowned when they were attempting to cross the river. One of the bodies, Jeremiah Jackson's, was found in the water at Chatershaugh, near Fatfield on January 15th, 1772.

John Etherington's mill and most of its contents at Cocken were swept away; Mr. Mowbray's corn stacks at Newbrough, a lot of Lumley boathouse's furniture and the fishing-lodge suffered the same fate.

Flood water surged 200 yards into Chester-le-Street and inundated the shops and houses.

View from Prebends Bridge (built in the 18th century to replace a footbridge swept away in 1771 flood) downstream to Grade I listed Framwellgate Bridge, Durham which was built across the River Wear in 1120 by Bishop Rannulf Flambard. (Bishop Thomas Langley ordered the construction of the present bridge which was widened in the 19th century.) The original structure of Framwellgate Bridge was damaged in floods in 1400 and in 1318 the Bishop's Steward, Richard Fitzmarmaduke, was murdered by his cousin, Ralph Neville on this bridge.

North Biddick, Low Lambton and Chatershaugh collieries were inundated with water causing the drowning of approximately thirty horses. Coal, houses, two fire engines and wagons were lost. Apparently all the low lying ground from Cocken to Chester-le-Street was littered with flood debris.

When the flood reached the sea at Sunderland a number of keels and thirty-four ships were wrecked. The cries of the boys aboard (most of the men were ashore) drove those on land to mount rescue attempts, but the rain and dark stopped many from receiving help. Keels were driven off by the elements and many men and boys lost their lives.

The sheer force of water broke down the pier at one point and at another when numerous vessels were driven into it. The following morning the harbour was full of floating hay stacks, furniture and a staith (a platform for landing coal). Sadly, eight or nine bodies were also on the harbour's shore.

Then there was the River Tees.

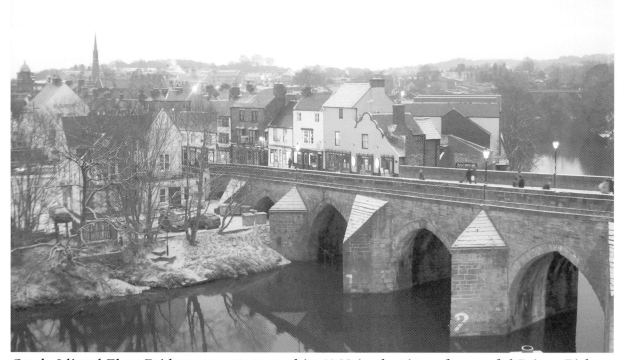

Grade I listed Elvet Bridge was constructed in 1160 in the time of powerful Prince Bishop Hugh de Puiset, known as 'Bishop Pudsey'. It spans the River Wear at Durham. One arch is 12th century the others are 13th century. Three arches were destroyed in the flood in 1771.

The Tees

High Force, spewed flood water 69ft to the ground and was apparently a sight to behold.

Downstream, Barnard Castle came off worst. The arch of the bridge couldn't withstand the pressure of the water which demolished the battlement. Water gushed down the street; ruined the causeway; shifted soil leaving rock in its wake and destroyed eight houses, leaving nothing standing.

The original bridge was left 4ft higher than the rock as the surrounding land had been washed away. Those travelling to Yorkshire had to use a ladder to climb onto the bridge!

A dyer, who was working in a cellar, left a few pieces of '*tammies*' (rough cloth with a tight weave, traditionally used to strain soups and sauces) in a kettle, in his rush to get out. On returning when the water had subsided, he removed mud and sand from the kettle and discovered the 'tammies' were an unexpected colour: blood red. This was probably caused by deposits of iron-oxide in the water. He sent the goods to London and was immediately given another order for more of the same hue. Unfortunately, despite numerous attempts, he couldn't replicate it.

Croft and Darlington didn't escape; the flood also caused damage here.

High Force is England's biggest waterfall and the drop is a spectacular 70ft into a plunge pool. The rock at the top is Whin Sill.

Yarm was inundated by fifteen feet of water. People had to climb onto the roofs of their homes to await rescue by boat. Ann Richardson sat for fifteen hours with a child in her arms before she was rescued.

Stockton had never experienced flooding like this before. Fortunately, the water only submerged two or three cellars and a warehouse. (*Sykes, Vol.1, p.43, 285, 287*)

Water does not only flow, it can also freeze. We've all heard of London's medieval Frost Fair on the Thames, but have you heard what happened in Newcastle?

Ice

During the '*Little Ice Age*' between the 15th and 19th centuries in Northern Europe, rivers like the Tyne froze over. Conditions needed to be cold and dry for a long time. First the area near river banks and bridges would form ice patches which met and grew till the surface of the rivers had frozen. When the ice appeared thick enough, Frost Fairs involving eating, drinking, dancing and winter games would be held. The freeze could last as long as three months.

The first recorded Frost Fair was in London in 1564 and attracted thousands to venture onto the ice. People played football, held archery contests, feasted and danced. London's 1814 Frost Fair is known as the biggest as stalls and booths were erected on the Thames; there were donkey rides and a sheep was roasted.

There is an account of water freezing on the River Tyne, on January 14th,

Ice on the River Tyne in the 1960s.

1773, for about four miles below the Tyne Bridge in Newcastle. Apparently hundreds of people ventured on to the ice and enjoyed skating and sliding on it. The ice didn't have the same consistency of thickness above the bridge and therefore was viewed as unsafe. Concern was expressed about what the movement of the ice was doing to the piles supporting the temporary wooden bridge. A number of workmen were employed to break up and remove the chunks of ice around them.

Four days later, oblivious to any danger, two young men skated against a given time of 16 minutes, racing up and down the Tyne for three miles below the bridge. It took them 15 minutes.

Another account says that the river also froze for four miles below the bridge on January 18th, 1774 and that it took two men, 15 minutes to skate six miles.

On January 26th, 1776, following a sustained fall of snow on Newcastle and its surroundings, the temperature dropped to below freezing and the Tyne froze from Newburn to approximately two miles below the bridge. Hundreds of people walked and skated on the river. They were the lucky ones.

Some roads were impassable because of snow drifts and two women became so tired and cold when travelling from Newcastle Market, they sheltered in a house on the way to Loosing Hill, near Whickham, County Durham. They died within hours!

Worse was to come. Later that day, on the moors between Morton and Trimdon, a fisherman's corpse was discovered in the snow. Ralph of Winlaton, a well know seller of walking sticks and rods, died in the snow between Winlaton and Swalwell and on the same night, two farmers making their way from Newcastle to Earsdon died on Killingworth Moor.

Three days later, when hundreds of men were clearing snow and ice from the Morpeth, Ponteland and Shields turn-pike roads, a saddle and a dead horse were found.

January 15th, 1814

A Dutch sailor tested the frozen Tyne by using a pole and skating with beef bones tied to his shoes. Keelmen were paid to sweep the ice, as they had been laid off work because of the frost. A number of expert skaters were noted, for example Cuthbert Ellison, Esq. M.P. for Newcastle, but snow fell making skating impracticable, followed by rain and a drop in temperature.

There was then a Frost Fair for several days on the frozen Tyne sometimes lasting into the night. Apparently it was similar to a race-ground or country fair. Fires were lit; and booths sold alcohol. Sellers of fruit and cakes hawked their wares; razor-grinders sought customers and recruiting parties hunted for possible soldier material, whilst fiddlers and pipers played. There were a number of races with or without skates for prizes such as clothing and in one instance, a leg of mutton. A horse and sledge were even brought onto the frozen river. The ice finally thawed on Sunday, February 6th, 1814.

Fortunately there appears to be no record of disasters at the Frost Fairs but, when water thaws it can cause rapid flooding.

December 30th, 1815 – Thaw!

There was a rapid thaw accompanied by wind and rain. The River Tyne overflowed its banks and flooded the Quayside and the Close. One vessel, the Carlisle London trader, was moored to a cannon. The trader was torn away, cast adrift, but later secured. Anchors from most ships at the Quay were later found hooked into the pavement.

'A keel got fixed length wise across the second arch from the north of the bridge, when the cries of the keelmen induced a man and a spirited youth to put off in a boat for their rescue. On returning from the keelmen, the boat was swamped; and though the keelmen were saved, the rescuers were drowned.' (Mackenzie, 1827)

Fire

Flooding wasn't the only hazard. Fire was equally feared. In the Middle Ages fire fighting arrangements were haphazard and ineffective. It was only in 1666, with the catastrophic results of the Great Fire of London, that urban fire fighting was standardised. Nicholas Broom, a property developer, introduced the first insurance against fire and formed the first fire brigade. Others followed, but to counter fraud, policy holders were given a brightly coloured fire mark or badge to affix between the first and ground floor windows.

Fires were caused by numerous factors such as the density of wooden housing, the weather, accidents or arson.

In the 17th century fires were fought with basic equipment such as a fire engine, buckets, ladders, shovels, scoops, fire hooks and gunpowder! Health and Safety didn't appear to have been considered.

Health and Safety must have been the last things on the

An early fire brigade at Ryhope, County Durham, 1910.

minds of the congregation celebrating Matins (a service) in Durham Cathedral on Corpus Christi Day in 1429. Corpus Christi is Latin for the body of Christ and the day was also known as the most Holy Body of Christ and the Day of Wreaths. It's a feast in the Christian calendar honouring the Holy Eucharist, the Last Supper. No longer a public holiday in England, Corpus Christi, was celebrated by City Guilds in processions and by plays. Taking place somewhere between May 21st and June 24th, this particular Corpus Christi Day must have been a memorable experience for those in and outside Durham Cathedral.

1429 – Fire in the Belfry

On Corpus Christi Day, during Matins at Durham Cathedral, the belfry was struck by lightning which set the cathedral alight! After a number of hours, about twenty feet of the burning belfry, its iron work and timber crashed down onto the church.

It wasn't only cathedrals that had fires, castles had them too.

Haggerston Castle's Curse

Haggerston Castle in Northumberland is located 5 miles south of Berwick-upon-Tweed. Built to subdue the local peasants and keep the Scots out of England, it was partially destroyed by fire in 1618 and again in 1911 and went from being a 14th century castle to 21st century caravan park. According to legend, the castle was cursed by a witch and she is blamed for the fires.

The castle was first mentioned in records when Edward II visited in 1311 and was described as '*strong*' in 1345.

Durham Cathedral.

The de Hagardestons, were probably part of William the Conqueror's army. The land was wet and boggy then. Unfortunately, there are few early records remaining as documents were destroyed in fires. In the late 12th and early 13th centuries, a John de Hagardeston lived in the castle. The Hagardestons or Haggerstons (the name was anglicized in the 15th century) married well and owned large tracts of land. Later owners were the Maxwell and Naylor families.

The centuries took their toll, because in 1772 the castle was a ruin and in 1805 it was partially pulled down and a house built in its place. The house was later raised to the ground leaving an L-plan tower which became a water tower and a belvedere (a lookout or viewpoint). In 1933 the estate went under the auctioneer's hammer as 2,000 lots were up for sale. It's now a caravan park set in 256 acres.

Castles were built to subdue the local populace and for defence in time of war, on the other hand religious buildings were conceived for worship by men of God. In medieval times, travellers on journeys between religious establishments were called pilgrims, hence the name Pilgrim Street in Newcastle. It led to and from the medieval bridge into town. Those who pass along it now would be shocked at the deprivation and poverty of 18th century Newcastle and the fate of a child who lived there.

June 13th, 1744 – The Woman who Lived in a Hole

Ann Potts and her child lived in a hole in Pilgrim Street, Newcastle. She was drunk when a candle set alight to the straw on which she and her child were lying. Unfortunately the infant burnt to death.

Another ancient street in Newcastle was The Close, (running one street back and parallel to the Quayside). It was narrow and confined, when it was originally built, though the first prosperous owners lived in large, comfortable homes. However, increasing industrialisation with its noise, smells and pollution in the late 18th century forced residents to move out. Perhaps it was just as well. As can be seen by several incidents below, living cheek by jowl beside businesses in wooden premises using or containing combustible material, was not perhaps the best of ideas.

The Great Fire of London in 1666 is famous all over the world, but there were numerous fires in the North East

Pilgrim Street Gate, Newcastle.

and one particularly destructive one in Newcastle in 1750.

July 24th, 1750 – The Great Fire of Newcastle

The fire started at 11pm in a merchant's cellar used as a warehouse, at the bottom of an entry to the Close in Newcastle. The area was full of densely packed buildings and there was no quay or wharf between them and the Tyne.

The probable cause was a heated brewer's copper in an inn-keeper's brew house which adjoined the merchant's cellar. The shared brick wall overheated causing some of the merchant's combustible goods to ignite. The flames sped through the cellar and into the open, before the fire was discovered.

Mr. Martin Bryson was a well known bookseller and lived above the cellar where he kept a stock of books. Fortunately, he wasn't at home, but his servants narrowly escaped with their lives as the floors gave way just after they jumped out of their beds. By this time many of the people of Newcastle were aware of the fire and offered assistance. Unfortunately, the narrow street, congested housing and the close vicinity of the water worked against them.

Despite their endeavours to smother the approaching flames, roofs, chimneys and walls of neighbouring houses were raised to the ground. Water and buckets were plentiful. The arrival of magistrates and deployment of Lord Ancram's regiment, quartered in Newcastle, proved invaluable. Buildings were emptied of furniture and goods and placed under armed guard.

Even so, by eight the next morning ten houses, goods, furniture and numerous warehouses had been destroyed. The fire caused £10,000 worth of damage. The good news was that £800 was raised to help the victims of the fire. A list was compiled and the money was distributed on March 18th, 1751 to the following: Mr. Martin Bryson, £70; Jonathan Haswell, a flax-dresser, £20; to deceased Mr. Benjamin Heslop's children, £370; Mr. James Hume, £30; Mrs. Katherine Jefferson, £8; Jonathan Pearson, servant to Mr. Harrison, £20; Robert Maclean, £8; Mr. John Shaw and his sister, £250 and to Margaret Young, servant of Mr. Bryson, £30.

They were lucky there was no wind, if there had been, Sandhill and possibly most of Newcastle would have burnt to the ground.

Sometimes fires are not caused by chance or accident; sometimes it's a deliberate act. Even in 1841, arson was considered a very serious crime alongside, murder, violent theft, wounding and sodomy. The perpetrators, once convicted, would have been sentenced to death, though many had their sentences commuted.

Mr. Barber must have been very anxious to catch those demanding money with menaces in 1773 as they would have been equally grateful to get away with the deed.

March 6th, 1773 – The Case of the Incendiary Letters

A fire destroyed the house of Mr. Barber at Summerhill, Newcastle. It started at about 2am and went on for four hours. Suspicion rests on the anonymous writer of '*two incendiary*' letters Barber had received at an earlier date, demanding money be left on his garden wall. Although a reward of £110 and a King's pardon was offered, the offenders were not caught.

The park at Summerhill, Newcastle.

Sometimes fires can be started by a hazard that can't be smelled, heard or seen. Striking without warning, the results can be devastating. The simultaneous presence of three elements is required: fuel such as sugar, oxygen and a spark. Even in the 21st century there have been tragic incidents concerning combustible dust. I'm not sure Messrs. Forster and Co. in 1785 would have been consoled by that.

September 8th, 1785 – Sugar-House Fire

Messrs. Forster and Co. had a huge sugar-house which fronted the river in the Close, Newcastle. It was seen to be ablaze just before midnight. The fire bell was rung and all of Newcastle's fire engines arrived. By 2am flames were shooting out of several windows, but the firemen and locals worked together to try to prevent the fire spreading to other buildings.

Despite all their exertions, within hours, the whole of the sugar-house, and most of its valuable contents along with Mr. Clapham's adjoining brewery were reduced to ashes. Buildings opposite were also considerably damaged.

Occasionally, a fire has no obvious cause, though an open, unguarded fire, oil lamp or candle flame can never be ruled out. Perhaps this was the case in the Bigg Market in 1791.

March 16th, 1791 – Bigg Market Fire

It was about midnight when Mr. Powell, a surgeon, and his family in the Bigg Market woke and became aware that their their house was on fire. They managed to scramble out just in time, but all their valuable furniture and the house were consumed by the flames.

Often the cause of a fire is all too obvious. Living close to 18th century paint had its dangers as it contained white lead, linseed oil and organic pigments. Linseed oil is combustible. When it dries through oxidation, heat is released and the faster it dries, the greater the heat. A pile of rags covered in linseed oil can instantaneously combust without warning. Is this what happened in the Pudding Chare fire?

July 10th, 1816 – Pudding Chare Fire

It was midnight when a fire broke out on the upper floors of premises in Pudding Chare, Newcastle. There were two inhabitants: Mr. Lawson, a currier (curriers dressed, finished and coloured properly tanned hides) and Mr. Beeney, a painter and glazier. Mr. Lawson's shop and Mr. Beeney's varnishing room were both threatened by flames. They were so high and intense that two houses adjoining and fronting the Bigg Market were also at risk.

By 2am, the fire was out and any damage was limited to the original site. Fortunately Mr. Lawson and Mr. Richardson, the owner of the building were both insured. Poor Mr. Beeney was not.

Glass making also had its hazards as a furnace would have been used.

August 9th, 1821 – Glass Company Goes Up in Smoke

The premises of the Northumberland Glass Company fronted the Close, Newcastle. It had extensive buildings and warehouses. A fire broke out at about 1am and it spread so rapidly that an hour later most of the establishment was afire and most of the stock was destroyed. All that remained was the cone of the furnace, near the River Tyne. A number of *'labouring'* families in adjoining houses almost lost their belongings as well as lives.

In imminent danger from the fire, were soap manufacturer's Messrs. Doubleday and Co's counting house and The Mansion House. They were located close to the Glass Company, on the east side and in danger from the flames and sparks.

Sparks were landing on a large number of barrels of rosin out in the open in a yard near The Mansion House. Rosin is a solid form of resin found in pines and is highly flammable and potentially explosive. The barrels were hurriedly rolled into the street and men with buckets of water told to stand by.

Messrs. Doubleday and Co. on the west side of the Glass Company then caught fire, but a west wind carried the flames in the opposite direction.

By 5am the fire was contained, smouldered most of the day and eventually burnt itself out in the Glass Company's buildings. (*Mackenzie; Sykes, Vol. 2, p.139-140*)

Newcastle in the 1820s – Close Gate.

40

Wood and paper were also highly flammable.

August 9th, 1813 – Westgate Street Fire

Messrs. Goodlad and Co was a paper manufactory business, located in a yard, facing the Cross-house, in Westgate Street. The business occupied a section of the second and upper floors of the building which, with its contents, was devastated by a fire which broke out at 6pm.

Coachmaker, Mr. Hodgson, whose work-shop was on the second floor, *'suffered considerable loss.'*

Mr. Pearson owned the whole building. His dry salting premises, stable and several warehouses, were also badly damaged. (*Sykes, Vol.2, p.74*)

It wasn't just factories that were in danger of catching fire, places of entertainment were also at risk.

Fires at Newcastle's Theatre Royal

On February 19th, 1823 Newcastle's Theatre Royal in Drury Lane, was lit by gas. The audience was watching 'Tom and Jerry' when apparently, gas from a pipe in one of the lower boxes near the stage produced smoke and flames in the gallery.

Despite being informed there was no danger as the fire had been almost immediately extinguished, those in the gallery weren't convinced and rushed to get out. The cry of, *'Fire, fire – save your lives!'* did not help. Eight people were trodden to death, others suffocated. Amongst the dead were: Mr. John Edwards, a cellarman from Gateshead; Mr. Handyside, a bookbinder's son; Dorothy Heaton, 17 year old daughter of tailor, Mr. George Heaton; 16 year old milliner, Mary Johnson; 19 year old, Isabella Parkinson, adopted child of Mrs. Green of Pilgrim Street; John Jonathan Wilkinson, son of a veterinary surgeon from Pilgrim Street and Mrs. Riddell Robson who died in her injured husband's arms. Several people were hurt. It would have been worse if the check-taker had opened the upper barrier as more people would have been killed.

This wasn't the worst fire experienced by the Theatre Royal. In 1837 the theatre moved to Grey Street. Strangely, Mr. Jolland, one of the last to leave the theatre on November 23rd, 1899, noticed nothing unusual at 11.30pm and neither did a police constable on his rounds an hour later.

The Theatre Royal in 1804.

Despite these accounts, a passerby reported smoke coming from the building in the early hours of November 24th. The police and fire brigade were called, but for some reason no steam fire-engine arrived for one and half hours.

When firemen broke into the theatre, the stage was alight; dressing rooms were in flames and the fire was spreading to the roof. An attempt was made to save the premises adjoining the theatre.

Disasters often attract crowds. Even though it was 2am, an odd assortment of people gathered. Some were in ball gowns and evening wear, returning home from an evening dancing, others were poorly dressed and some had been woken by the police because of the danger and were in night wear. By 3am flames could be seen along the theatre's roof, but the fire was contained.

Once the flames had been extinguished, the scene was one of a charred, blackened ruin. The structural walls remained, but only the back of the auditorium was untouched. The proscenium and most of the auditorium were wrecked. Private boxes were destroyed; rafters and beams were scorched and the dome had crashed to the ground. Fortunately the safe and office books had been saved by Mr. Lingham and Mr. Benson.

Land was purchased on either side of the gutted building and the Theatre Royal rose from the ashes to reopen on Tuesday, December 31st, 1901 with a production of 'The Forty Thieves'.

A Theatre Royal ticket from the 1970s when a seat for the back stalls cost 75p.

Right: A Theatre Royal programme from 1951 with the 1901 building on the front cover. The programme was for a performance of 'Othello' with Orson Welles in the title role.

The Theatre Royal after a snow storm in 1886.

Explosions

We don't expect explosions in buildings in close proximity to our homes. The Side has its origins as a medieval street where people lived, shopped and travelled to and from Newcastle's only bridge. It would be interesting to hear what contemporary Health and Safety experts thought of the goings on there in 1799.

August 28th, 1799 – Explosive News

Mr. Bulman, a saddler and ironmonger, had a warehouse at the head of the Side, Newcastle. He must have been most alarmed to discover that it was on fire at 6am, especially when he knew he had gunpowder stored in the upper warehouse!

The fire bell was rung and a drum beat to arms. The arrival of water engines, local men and the military meant crowds could be kept back, pilfering was prevented and hopefully the fire extinguished.

Most of the stock was burnt, but some was saved, though a number of people were injured as they moved it to safety. Bulman, having told his assistants about the gunpowder, watched two brave men climb a ladder and somehow get the heated barrels into St. Nicholas' Church. I bet the vicar was pleased about that!

Although Bulman lost a lot of his stock, the fire was extinguished inside an hour. No one lived on the premises, and it wasn't obvious how the fire started. A fire had been lit for some hours the day before, but had apparently been put out at 6pm that evening.

The Side, Newcastle, around 1900.

Being involved in an accident at work is one thing, but most of us expect to be safe in our own homes. Modern statistics don't bear this out. There are in fact more accidents at home than anywhere else.

Those of us who have gas piped into our homes, don't give it a thought until we cook, heat our water and or use it to warm us. But even in the 21st century there have been gas explosions causing loss of life. The warning was there almost 200 years ago.

January 6th, 1821 – Gas Explosion

' ... a dreadful explosion of gas took place in the house of Benjamin Slater, Forth Street, Newcastle. The upper part of his house and the whole back part of the one adjoining, were blown out and destroyed. Seven men and seven women were injured; and one child was killed.' (Mackenzie, 1827)

Extreme Weather

Most of us like to feel safe, but today we appear obsessed with climate change and the fear the world is heating up or cooling down. Extreme weather has always been with us, but sometimes the elements can combine with disastrous consequences, as it did on June 28th, 2012 and centuries earlier in January, 1742.

January 28th, 1742 – A Tempest

The wind had been gusting all day, but by evening it had worsened and thunder and lightning joined forces. Alderman Ridley's household in Westgate Street, Newcastle must have been shocked when the chimney crashed down making a great gash in the roof

Mr. Gray's house is recorded as having been, *'blown down and most of its contents destroyed'*. *(Sykes, Vol. 1, p.166-167)*

Westmoreland Place, Westgate Street, Newcastle, 1820s.

On the same day the Rising Sun Farm, near Killingworth, Northumberland, was struck by lightning and, because of the ferocity of the wind, burnt to ashes. The farm, owned by Messrs. Mather and Coulson, comprised a farmhouse, barns, stables, byers and stacks. The livestock, 22 animals in all, consisting of cows, horses and oxen were burnt to death. Fifteen corn stacks; twenty-two bolls (a Scotch measure) of corn and almost a hundred bolls of oats also went up in smoke. How many businesses could afford this sort of loss?

On the Killingworth road, riders found their horses had their manes and tails singed and one person reported his whip struck several times by lightning, though he was unhurt.

At eight o'clock, Captain Hammond, from Yarmouth, must have watched in horror as a tremendous flash of lightning set fire to the sails and masts of his ship which was moored on the Tyne. The vessel was completely destroyed. The spring tide meant the current in the river was strong and in Shields several ships broke away from their moorings and were damaged.

Lightning was feared and it wasn't until 1752 when American, Benjamin Franklin proved it was a form of electricity and invented the lightning rod. However, if man or beast was caught in the open, there was little anyone could do.

The aftermath of a lightning strike on a road in Newcastle on June 28th, 2012. The Tyne Bridge was also hit that night.

The Coast Road at Heaton, Newcastle, is closed by the police after flooding in August, 2012.

February 1806 – Storm at Fair

Several cows and horses at the fair on Cowhill, Newcastle, were scorched with lightning, and one man with four horses was killed at Cowgate.

The old mill and inn at Cowgate, Newcastle, in the 1800s.

Why didn't David Sutton's house and a mill in 1809 have lightning rods?

August 3rd, 1809 – Thunderstorm

'An awful storm of thunder, lightning and hail passed over Newcastle.' Mr. David Sutton's house and furniture in Princes' Street were damaged as well as Mr. Francis Humble's house, near the Forth.

The mill near St. Andrew's Church was set on fire and Mr. Hawke's in Jesmond experienced the melting of *'... the works of a gold watch, which was hanging up ...'* (*Sykes, Vol. 2, p.45-46*)

Shipwrecks

We may have heard of Grace Darling and her heroic rescue of some of the crew of the *Forfarshire*, wrecked on Big Harcar, one of the Farne Islands in September 1838, but have you heard about the lesser known, Bella Brown from Cresswell, Druridge Bay, Northumberland?

Newbiggin-by-the-Sea Lifeboat House built in 1851.

Bella, apparently witnessed a Swedish steamer the *Gustav* being driven onto rocks below Snab Point, on a stormy winter's night in 1876. Knowing the nearest life boat station was at Newbiggin-by-the-Sea, several miles south, she scrambled over rocks and waded waist high through water in the pitch black to get help. Thanks to her almost all the crew were saved.

The North East coast is littered with wrecked shipping. The infamous Black Middens rocks off the north bank of the mouth of the River Tyne claimed numerous ships. The black colour, perhaps reminded locals of old dumps which were used for domestic waste and could have contained vegetable matter; animal bones and human excrement and so on, hence the name Black Middens.

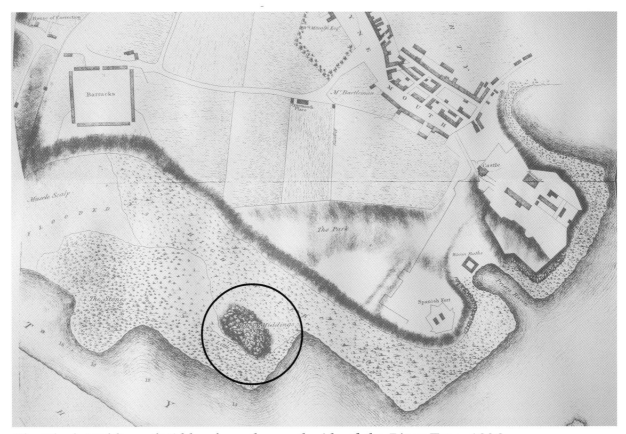

The Black Middings (Middens) on the north side of the River Tyne, 1826.

January 25th, 1794 – The Black Middens

The storm began with lightning, followed by a strong gale from the north. The church of St. Nicholas and several Gateshead churches lost their highest vanes. Three men were killed west of Newcastle on the military road and one man on Shields road. A number of coal keels on the river disappeared and five ships moored at Jarrow Slake were swept from their berths. There are differing accounts of the ships wrecked, but two were apparently driven on to Herd Sands, the *Barbara* from Shields, the *Hazard* from Sunderland and the *Alexander* and *Margaret* were wrecked on the Black Middens at the north side of the harbour. (*Mackenzie, 1827; Sykes, Vol.1, p.370*)

Just entering or leaving the Tyne, presented early ships' captains with numerous challenges. For instance, the river was so shallow that no vessel with a draught of more than 20ft was allowed to sail in or out. The river mouth was exposed to south-easterly and north-easterly gales, making sailing hazardous.

To gain the Narrows, the entrance to the river, captains had to navigate round a series of natural obstacles. For instance the river mouth was obstructed by the treacherous Tynemouth Bar. Records in 1782 show a minimum depth of 7ft at low tide on the bar and a similar depth at high water over the Herd Sands to the south of the river. Herd Sands, stretched a mile south to Trow Rocks and half a mile into the sea at its furthest point. Even then shipping wasn't safe. Low tide would reveal the Black Middens rocks and Mussel Scarp sands off Tynemouth on the north bank of the river.

Upriver there were various shallows close to the banks. Ballast was often deposited in the Tyne, despite penalties for doing this. This meant the river silted up.

In 1824 records show the Tyne as having quick-sands, dangerous sandbanks and shoals, as well as quantities of coal, stone, gravel, sand, soil, silt, mud and other substances in the river.

Marsden Bay: the twin piers at the mouth of the River Tyne are in the distance.

The river was so difficult to navigate by 1850 that the Tyne Navigation Act was passed, so the Tyne Improvement Commission took control of the river and a programme of dredging was begun. Before this, at low water spring tides, people had been known to wade across the river between South and North Shields. The dredging made the river and its entrance safer, but nothing could control the North Sea or the weather.

Up to the late 18th century, life at sea was an unpredictable and perilous occupation and so was any form of rescue.

Today approximately 1,300 lives are saved every year by lifeboats coming from the 220 lifeboat stations on our coast. They provide a 24 hour service up to 50 miles from the coast of the United Kingdom and the Republic of Ireland.

1786 – The First Innovation

The Royal National Lifeboat Institution recognises Lionel Lukin's 1786 adaptation as the first rescue boat to save lives. It was small, flat-bottomed and was first used for rescues off the Bamburgh coast, perhaps testimony to the North East weather.

1789 – The Competition to Design a Lifeboat

Three years later, in 1789, tragedy struck the crew of a Newcastle ship, the *Adventure* when a storm ran her aground at the mouth of the Tyne. Despite those ashore being able to see eight of the crew, no one would attempt a rescue in the suicidal conditions. The crew perished. Several local businessmen, a branch of The Coal Trade Group known as '*The Gentlemen of Lawe House*' in South Shields, were so shocked by the incident that they decided to advertise for the first purpose-built rescue boat.

'A reward of two guineas will be given to any person producing a plan (which shall be approved of by the committee appointed for that purpose, as the best) of a boat, capable of holding twenty-four persons, and calculated to go through a very shoal, heavy, broken sea. The intention being to preserve the lives of seamen, from ships coming ashore, in hard gales of wind. Plans will be received on any day, at the Lawe- House, South Shields, and the Committee will meet at three o'clock on the 10th of June, to determine who shall be entitled to the reward. The committee will be obliged to any Gentlemen favouring them with his hints, or sending them a plan to that day.'
(*Newcastle Courant, May 2nd, 1779*)

They received lots of letters, but only two models. One was designed by 41 year old Willie Wouldhave, a local parish clerk, and the other by 32 year old Henry Greathead, a boatbuilder.

Who won?

Who designed the first lifeboat was to become an ongoing contentious issue even to this day. At the suggestion of the chairman of the committee, Nicholas Fairles, Wouldhave was given half the prize money. Obviously put out, he refused to accept it at first, but records show that he was paid this sum. His boat with its self-righting properties and use of copper was possibly too innovative and it was rejected by the committee as being unsuitable for local conditions. His model did at least float. Greathead's model, rather ironically for a shipbuilder, sank!

They could have given up here because Fairles and his committee would have expected to have a design which met their criteria. They patently didn't, as they went on to gather suggestions from their competition letters, local pilots, fishermen and knowledgeable individuals. Then the committee produced a clay model to their own specifications. Sadly, none of Wouldhave's ideas were used.

The committee asked Greathead to build the boat and he added his own ideas to the design. This boat was unnamed, but eventually called the *Original*. Greathead appeared to forget he was working to the design specifications set out by the committee. It all seems to have gone to his head and thought perhaps there was money to be made if he could say he invented the first lifeboat. He wasn't wrong.

He approached numerous bodies with this claim. The Newcastle Literary and Philosophical Society awarded him five guineas; Trinity House gave him 100 guineas in 1802; he received 100 guineas from Lloyds of London which gave an additional £2,000 to create a fund to encourage the further building of lifeboats and in 1802 Parliament awarded him £1,200 for inventing the lifeboat!

The construction of the Wouldhave Monument in South Shields.

Wouldhave wasn't impressed and neither, I suspect was Fairles, who would only endorse a certificate that stated Greathead's model had entered the competition and from his explanations and design, was chosen to build the first boat. The curved keel was a later idea and not on his original model.

Today the Royal National Lifeboat Institution only recognises South Shield's boat builder Henry Greathead as the man who designed the first lifeboat for sea rescue.

The lives of Wouldhave, Greathead and Fairles didn't end well. In 1821 Wouldhave aged 70, died in poverty near the Mill Dam, South Shields.

Greathead became bankrupt, petitioned Parliament for more money and received £650, but by 1813 he was in a debtors' prison. He died in 1818 aged 63 and was buried in Limehouse, London.

Fairles, had the most unfortunate end of all. He became a magistrate and his name will be forever linked to miner, William Jobling, one of the last two men to be hanged and gibbeted in England. Jobling's crime? At the height of the miners' strike in the Durham and Northumberland coalfield, he held Fairles' horse, whilst his friend, Ralph Armstrong murdered Fairles near Jarrow Slake in 1832!

A plaque on the Wouldhave Monument that commemorates Queen Victoria's Jubilee in 1887 as well as the lifeboat first designed and built at South Shields in 1760.

1854 – The Royal National Lifeboat Institution

In 1842 Sir William Hillary, led a campaign for a National Institution for the Preservation of Life from Shipwreck, which in 1854 became the Royal National Lifeboat Institution.

1864 – The Tynemouth Volunteer Life Brigade

The Tynemouth Volunteer Life Brigade was first formed in 1864 to train men in the deployment of ship-to-shore rescue known as breeches buoy rescue. This involved a rocket with a line attached being fired over a ship and was invented by Henry Trengrouse, from Helston, Cornwall.

A lifeboat in rough seas off Tynemouth.

After witnessing the death of about 100 people aboard the Royal Navy 44-gun frigate, HMS *Anson*, at Loe Bar, off Cornwall in 1807, Trengrouse spent much of his life inventing the breeches buoy and saved countless lives. He died penniless, though not forgotten despite being rewarded with £20 from a grateful nation and 20 guineas from the Society of Arts.

How Breeches Buoy worked

The line was attached to the strongest part of the ship, usually the mast, and used to transfer three other lines aboard the stricken ship, one of them being the breeches buoy. This consisted of a pair of breeches or trousers with a flotation device attached, into which a member of the crew stepped to be hauled ashore by those on land, simple but highly effective.

For instance the schooner *Peggy* was wrecked on the Black Middens on October 13th, 1891. With a cargo of coal she'd left the Tyne only to meet hurricane force winds. The Tynemouth Brigade used breeches buoy and rescued four crewmen. On being told by the captain that a fifth man with a broken leg (he'd fallen out of the rigging when trying to get to the breeches buoy) was still on the wreck, Coastguard, officer George Hoar volunteered to save him.

After being hauled 150 yards through heavy seas, Hoar spotted the hawser attached 14ft above the deck and the unconscious man. Having returned ashore to confer with an officer, Hoar returned and eased the hawser which allowed him into the breeches buoy and access to the man. They were hauled ashore, the sea sometimes covering them, with Hoar's legs wrapped round the man's body and his two hands grabbing the man's coat collar. Hoar was awarded the Albert Medal of the second class by Queen Victoria for his bravery. Sometimes, however, severe conditions prevented rescue as was the case of the the *Burton* in 1832.

The *Burton* was a brig registered in Wivenhoe. Laden with coal, she sailed out of the Tyne on March 15th, 1865, but was driven back by bad weather on March 19th. Caught by the wind whilst avoiding two other ships, she was wrecked on the North Pier at the River Tyne. Despite a rocket line being fired, the vessel broke up before the crew could make it fast. Only one man was saved by lifeboat.

Training

There was an obvious need for crews to be trained in the use of breeches buoy. This was demonstrated by the events of December, 29th, 1865. Three ships came to grief because of a storm and southerly gale. The barque *Union* from Shoreham, and two brigs the *Levis* and *Wynyard* were under tow. When close to the Priory, they were stranded on Spar Hawk rocks near the Spanish Battery, Tynemouth. Lines (breeches buoy) were sent aboard, but the crews didn't know how to use them. The *Union* and *Levis* crews were eventually rescued by the lifeboat *Tyne*, and the *Wynyard* crew was rescued by the lifeboat *Willie Wake*. The crews were lucky.

Obviously attempting a rescue at sea, in darkness with poor visibility was extremely dangerous. It's unfortunate that in 1902 the Tynemouth Brigade hadn't access to an innovation which was to save lives later in 1905.

The Searchlight

On November 20th, 1902, the 1,022 ton Danish steamship *Knud* collided with another steamship the *Swaledale* off the Tyne and sank. Despite the presence of the Tynemouth lifeboat, seven drowned. This resulted in Mr. Roland Philipson Esq. presenting the Brigade with a searchlight.

Three years later the searchlight was used for the first time when the collier *Vauxhall* was leaving the Tyne. She collided with the *Broadmayne*, a large steamer carrying oil, which was sailing into the river. The *Vauxhall* suffered a rent to her bow. Despite the command to go full astern so she'd be beached, she started to do down by her bow. Her prop could be seen rotating clear of the water. The crew abandoned ship in the ship's boat. The *Vauxhall's* bulkheads collapsed after an hour and she settled, just clear of the shipping lanes, east of the Groyne.

Fourteen years later the searchlight was deployed again to successfully assist lifeboats in taking crew off the steamship *Linerton* which had run ashore at South Shields.

The Tyne Lifeboat

The lifeboat *Tyne* was in service from 1833-1882. Built by Oliver and Sons of South Shields she was presented by shipowner, Thomas Forrest. Stationed at Coble Landing, South Shields, alongside the *Providence*, she saved over 1,000 seaman. In one incident in particular in December 1849, she rescued 4 of the 24 *Providence* lifeboat crew who'd gone to the rescue of the capsized brig, *Betsy*. She was bombed in 1941, but has been preserved at the Wouldhave Memorial, South Shields.

The Tyne – the second oldest preserved lifeboat in Britain. Sometimes the weather is not at its best when men put out to sea.

Three Families Devastated

This story spans two centuries, devastating the Brown, Davison and Nicholson families from Blyth, Northumberland.

George and Thomas Brown's family had already been touched by tragedy when their father had drowned at sea some years before. But when George Brown placed his, *'For sale or hire'* advertisement in the *Blyth Bi Weekly News* on Friday, July 12th, 1895 he can't possibly have imagined there was more tragedy to come:

> *'For sale or hire. Sailing boat 'Marie'; in good order. –*
> *Apply George Brown. 39 Beaumont Street. Cowpen Quay.'*

George Brown was over thirty, a dredger workman, but he'd also been a seaman for over 15 years and owned the *Marie*, a sailing boat which he hired out so people could enjoy the bay at Blyth.

Setting off from Blyth on the morning of Saturday, July 13th, George headed north for Amble, but a heavy swell made him turn back. Described as, *'an expert handler of his craft'*, he set off again at 2pm, this time in squally weather with three men from Blyth.

Blyth Harbour entrance in the 1890s.

One of the men was George's brother Thomas, 21 a journeyman joiner. The second was 29 year old George Davison, a joiner, dredger workman, popular vocalist and father of four children. George Nicholson was the third man. At 22 years of age, he was an engineer on the dredger *Blyth*, a well known local footballer and youngest son of the harbour master. They were all athletic young men, but only one, Thomas Brown, was reputed to be a strong swimmer.

By Saturday evening concern was growing as there was no sign of the four men or their boat. The alarm was raised on the following day when the sea was running high and the *Marie* and the men still hadn't returned. A search was mounted. Several ports in the area were contacted by telegraph and a large yacht and two tugs combed the sea, but nothing was found.

Had the men been picked up by a *'passing steamer'* and perhaps put ashore on the coast? A steamer arriving in the Tyne reported sighting the hull of a boat drifting off Blyth, though another report of an overturned boat with the name *Marie* off St. Mary's Island was just one of many, *'sightings'* which were at first discounted.

Rumours abounded, but one in particular seemed to strike a chord. At between four and 5 o'clock a worker on a dredger reported that he'd seen, *'a sailing craft making heavy work getting in the direction of Blyth'*. He'd turned away for a moment, but when he'd looked again, the craft was nowhere in sight. He assumed the sail had been taken down or, ominously, that she'd, *'suddenly disappeared.'*

With no news of the men by July 16th it was generally assumed they'd drowned off St. Mary's Island, but strangely there was no sign of wreckage or bodies washed ashore. False stories of the boat being picked up and bodies recovered, circulated Blyth, much to the distress of all concerned.

The coast was on alert and friends of the men offered a reward for the recovery of the bodies. When the master of the steam tug *Defiance* arrived at Shields harbour he brought vital information and evidence. The *Defiance* had been 18 miles east-south-east of Tynemouth, when they'd sighted an upturned boat. The sails were reefed and it had

St. Mary's Island, Whitley Bay.

broken in two when they'd tried to right it. But they'd managed to secure the stern and haul it to Shields. The wooden timbers bore the name *Marie*.

Twelve days after the accident, George Davison's body, the head and face disfigured, was washed up on Blyth sands, near Hartley. Dressed in a light suit of clothes, the tide left him with his feet facing the sea on a bank directly opposite the Boiling Well Inn. Miner, Jon Elder from Seaton Sluice, found him. P.C. Armstrong searched George's pockets and found a tobacco pipe, a knife and half a crown in the left pocket. Apparently the dead man's appearance was *'shocking'*. George's sister identified him and his body was taken to the dead house in Seaton Sluice. His, father, Matthias, also a joiner, identified him at the inquest held at the Melton Constable Inn, Seaton Sluice.

The Melton Constable, Seaton Sluice, was built in 1839. Public Houses were routinely used for inquests.

The jury returned a verdict of, *'Accidental Drowning.'*

At the same time as George Davison's corpse was found, a second cadaver was sighted floating out at sea. Almost a week went by before George Brown's, *'shockingly decomposed body'* was discovered east of Blyth pier and towed ashore by Thomas Hatherick, a miner, who'd been fishing for mackerel.

Robert Brown identified his brother, George, by the clothes he was wearing. At the inquest held at the Ridley Arms the verdict was,

'Accidental Drowning.' For recovering the body, Hatherick was awarded 5s. from the coroner and another reward of £3. However, he suggested that he'd give £2 to the Davison Relief Fund.

It was to be another five days before Thomas Brown was found floating off the coast at Sunderland by fisherman Stephen Holmes. Robert Brown again had the sad duty of only being able to recognise a brother by his clothes. Thomas was 5ft 6ins and wore a red and blue striped shirt, gray tweed trousers, brown socks and laced boots. The jury returned the verdict, *'Accidentally Drowned'.*

On Thursday, August 22nd, forty days after they set sail, the sea gave up the last of the men. Apparently at between 4 and 5pm a corpse was discovered floating two miles off the Tyne. Two foyboatmen (they moored and cast off ships in the river) from South Shields, towed a body into Tynemouth Haven. Sergeant Weatherburn sent the severely decomposed body to the dead house at the Haven. A locket attached to a watch and 3s 4d were discovered in a pocket. The locket bore the inscription: *'G. Nicholson, won the Blyth Challenge Cup, 1894'.* The last of the men had come home.

George Nicholson's inquest was held at the Divisional Police Station, Tynemouth. His brother Robert identified him. George's rusty watch had stopped at 1.55pm. However, this gave no indication of when they capsized, as evidence was given that the watch had been broken before they set sail. The verdict of, *'Found drowned at sea'* was returned. All four men were buried at Blyth Cemetery. Sadly, Nicholson's handkerchief, bearing his full name, was later found tangled in a fishing line.

Those who lived in Blyth and had followed the story to its tragic end didn't forget George Davison's widow Margaret and their four children. The Davison Relief Fund was set up and through public subscriptions and a concert, held at Mr. Bertram's 'Blyth Circus of Varieties'. 1,400 tickets were sold and a total of £30 12s 9d collected and invested on behalf of the family. Money for the bereaved was also raised by the sale of memorial glasses, featuring the drowned men's names and an etching of the boat as seen below.

All four men are buried at Blyth Links Cemetery.

Far left: Photograph of memorial glass with the men's names etched on it.

Left: Memorial glass with etching of the pleasure boat.

Photographs taken with the kind permission of the Davison family.

A poignant footnote is the report in a local newspaper almost 22 years to the day of the 1895 drownings. It mentions a George Davison who lost his life on July 9th, 1917 when there was an internal explosion on HMS *Vanguard*. He was the son of the late George Davison who lost his life with three others in the boating accident of 1895.

(Blyth Bi Weekly News, Blyth News, The Evening Chronicle and Wansbeck Telegraph)

Disasters didn't just happen at sea, they also happened on land. The following tragedy changed the law.

1883 – The Victoria Hall Disaster

If you were a child in Sunderland in 1883, and given a ticket for, 'THE GREATEST TREAT FOR CHILDREN EVER GIVEN' and the word 'PRIZES' was mentioned, wouldn't you have wanted to go? And if you were the parent, wouldn't you have let him or her?

The Fays

The Fays were travelling entertainers and trawled local schools advertising an afternoon's entertainment and giving out tickets:

VICTORIA HALL, Sunderland
On Saturday Afternoon at 3 o'clock
SCHOOL TICKET
THE FAYS
From Tynemouth Aquarium
Will give a Good Day Performance for Children
THE GREATEST TREAT FOR CHILDREN EVER GIVEN
Conjuring, Talking Waxworks, Living
Marionettes, The Great Illusion, &c.
This Ticket will admit any number of children,
On payment of
ONE PENNY EACH; Reserved Seats, 2d; Nurses
Or Parents with Children 3d.
PRIZES!
Every child entering the room will stand a chance of receiving a handsome Present,
Books, Toys &c.
This Entertainment has been witnessed by
Thousands of
Delighted children throughout England.

Approximately 2,000 tickets were handed out. The Fays said that when the entertainment was finished, children with certain numbered tickets would receive a prize.

The Venue

Victoria Hall was a Gothic building facing Mowbray Park and standing at the junction of Laura Street and Toward Street. It was built in 1872 and had three floors: a ground floor – 'the pit'; a dress circle on the first floor and a gallery on the second floor.

The Audience

According to *The Times*, the hall held 3,500. On June 16th, the afternoon of the 'GREATEST TREAT' one woman and child sat in the dress circle; the gallery was full of young children and the pit was overflowing. At the inquest, Alexander Fay stated there were 20 adults and 1,050 children in the gallery.

The Tragedy

At the end of the performance The Fays finished with the *'hat trick'* where they announced children with certain numbers on their tickets had won a prize, pulled some prizes from a hat, and threw them into the pit. The winners in the gallery probably thought that by the time they got to the ground floor, all the prizes would be gone. Rushing out through folding doors, the children raced down 22 steps and turned left into first floor corridor with an entrance to the dress circle. They sped down 14 steps to turn tight left to a 12ft square landing and door leading to the lobby. The door was only open about 18-22 inches and was fastened by a bolt to the floor. The aperture allowed one person to pass through at a time, so tickets could be checked and money taken.

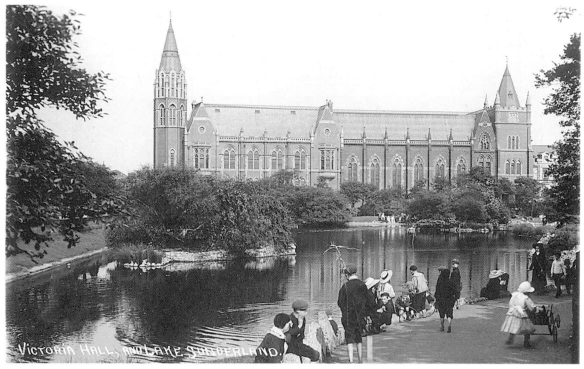

Victoria Hall with children playing in the foreground in Mowbray Park.

It can only be presumed that one or two children became stuck in the exit and the pressure of more and more children rushing down the stairs, many unable to see because of a turn in the stairs, caused children to be crushed, fall head over heels, pile one on top of another up to 6ft in height and the fourth step and suffocate. No screams were heard by the audience or outside in the street.

It's difficult to accept the death of a child, but the death of almost 200 aged from 3 to 14 years old in one afternoon defies the imagination. The tragedy that occurred in Sunderland's Victoria Hall on the June 16th, 1883 was reported all over the world. Queen Victoria was informed and sent a donation of £50 to the memorial fund.

Two inquests were held one after another: One at the Palatine Hotel, Sunderland for children born south of the River Wear and another at The Royal Hotel, Monkwearmouth for those born north of it.

The manager of the hall, Mr. Frederick Graham described what happened:

'It is my custom to give an eye to the gallery stairs, and to all the outlets when an audience is leaving the house and as I thought the entertainment was about to close I went towards the gallery stairs. When I approached the lower door I heard the fearful screams, groans, and voices of struggling. I rushed to the door and attempted to open it, and found I could not do so, the bolt was in the socket, about 2ft from the door frame, and the opening was jammed up nearly as high as my head with the bodies of children...' He went on to say, *'... I began by picking out those little ones from the top who groaned, moved their limbs or showed other signs of life ...'*

He added that the bodies were wedged 8ft deep and it was difficult to get to them, but he managed to hand children through a window to PC. Bewick. He placed them in the porch in the open air. Graham said he and his wife brought about eleven bruised and partially suffocated children back to consciousness.

More Help Arrived

Several doctors were then summoned and as a child was taken off the heap, they were medically examined. If alive, attempts were made to get them to regain consciousness. If they were dead they were taken to the body of the hall and placed in rows or laid in the lobby of the dress circle or principal lobby. The floor of the landing was strewn with caps, gloves and torn clothing. Some survivors were taken to Mr. Pott's house; fourteen were carried to the Palatine Hotel where they were treated by doctors and others were taken to the Sunderland Infirmary. As news of the disaster spread, passers-by and frantic parents gathered at the scene. Apart from the police, the Durham Regiment, the old 68th, were called to hold back the crowds.

The Parents

When parents were allowed through the cordon, they rushed into the hall. Parents burst into hysterics on finding their dead child and some women fainted. One man shouted, *'My son is dead – my son is dead! I will never go home – never no more!'* He rushed out, followed by those who were concerned about his personal safety.

Some parents, in their distress, recognised a jacket or scarf and misidentified a child, only to start the dreadful process again.

Cabs worked for nothing until 11pm, taking parents and their dead child or children home. Some, in their grief, misidentified a body, found their son or daughter alive at home and had to return to the hall with the body of someone else's child.

Approximately 183-190 children died. It's difficult to be precise as no lists were made before parents took their children away. Some families lost all their children; the Mills family lost four; over a dozen families lost two or more and 30 members of the same Sunday School class died. Three cemeteries were used and funerals took place from the following Tuesday to Friday. However, there were miraculous tales of survival.

Queen Victoria sent her sympathies.

Survivors' Tales

A boy with the surname of Souter, from Tunstall Road, told how he was in the gallery and was one of the last to go downstairs. He heard a noise and thought a row was going to begin. When a man opened another door, he ran to it and got out.

Mr. and Mrs. Wright's 11 year old daughter who was in the gallery said, *'I thought there was murder going on by the shouting I heard, and I came downstairs and got out another way ...'*

Maggie Gills saved herself by gripping a hand rail, and disabled Inez Coe wedged her crutch at an angle in front of herself, so she wasn't crushed.

Dr. Abrath arrived at the hall an hour after the disaster and discovered Ada Smith, a patient from his surgery, in extremis. He took her to the 'Hospital for Foreign Seamen' and, *'by means of electricity succeeded in sustaining the action of her heart.'*

Who was responsible?

Mr. Fay informed the inquest he'd not asked the police for help before the performance, despite the number of children. Mr. Wybert, his manager and Mr. Rain looked after the front entrance. Mr. Fay said he didn't even know the fatal door existed. However, he said just before the last trick, Mr. Wybert, *'saw that all the doors were right.'* Now what did that mean? The Fays and their manager did make some fatal errors. By charging more for a child accompanied by an adult, they ensured the majority of the audience would be children; they didn't provide enough staff and didn't visit the hall beforehand.

Fay added Mr. Hesseltine, his assistant, and Wybert left to see the children out at the end of the performance and Hesseltine took the box of presents with him. Fay also said it was Hesseltine who gave the first intimation that something was wrong when he fainted and being brought round with a drink of water said, *'Oh dear! There's some of them stuck fast, and they are dead.'* Did Hesseltine or Wybert use the bolt on the door, thus restricting the exit? Or was it Mr. Rain?

Tellingly, injured survivor, 9 year old Thomas Kent, informed the inquest he saw the man with the prizes (Hesseltine) trying to get through the gallery door, pull it a bit and put the bolt down.

According to hall-keeper, Frederick Graham, he and his wife had volunteered to help Mr. Fay, but said those who booked the hall were expected, *'to see to the safe seating of the people and safe egress at the close.'* Graham stated he hadn't shown Mr. Fay the door before June 16th and said he'd seen, *'the fatal door at half past 4 o'clock from the gallery steps and it was in its proper position.'* He added that after the disaster he'd tested the bolt 20 times and it hadn't slipped down and held the door in place, the inference being that the position of the bolt wasn't an accident.

When called back to the inquest, Graham didn't agree that it was *'reasonable'* those who'd booked the hall, should be shown over it. He said the building, had been re-examined by the borough surveyor eight months before and there'd been no comment about the exit.

Stephen Coates, clerk, was called by the inquest. He said he'd asked Mr. Fay how many staff he had and received the reply, *'Ample.'* He also said he'd advised Mr. Fay, *'...not to use the gallery as the children would be difficult to look after.'*

Mr. Frederick Taylor, the hall's owner agreed those, *'who made special profit should take a share of the responsibility.'* He added that the architect, Mr. Hoskins had nothing to do with the door as the hall's directors had ordered it to be erected. The door hadn't caused any problems before, but he believed, *'some change would be desirable.'*

The Children's Monument, Sunderland Park.

The Memorial to the children with Victoria Hall in the background. The Hall was destroyed during an air raid in the Second World War. The Memorial still stands in Mowbray Park

Had people been slipping in and out, whilst not paying for a ticket? Was profit the motive behind the directors' decision to restrict the size of the fatal exit? *The Graphic* made the point that there was, *'... a socket in the boards for the bolt to fit into ...'* and that this was, *'highly suggestive of a contrivance for the convenience of money-takers.'* Shouldn't Graham and his directors have consulted the architect and considered the safety of their audiences when altering the interior fittings of the hall? Shouldn't they have issued instructions that those who booked the hall, had to be shown all its exits and entrances?

The most burning question was whose hand pulled the bolt into position, thus narrowing the exit? Those with the most to gain undoubtedly had the best motive. Graham, the hall-keeper would have been paid anyway. If he's to be believed the door wasn't bolted at 4pm when The Fays were on stage. This leaves Rain, Hesseltine or Wybert especially if they had a share in the profits. The most likely candidate was Hasseltine as he was holding the prizes and Thomas Kent said he'd *'distinctly'* seen such a man pull the bolt down on the door.

There was a public outcry when the inquests found no one to blame. A second enquiry was called, but also failed to find who was responsible for bolting the exit door.

We have a tendency to joke about 'elf 'n' safety' today, but because of this tragedy, Parliament made it law that all places of public entertainment had to have enough exits, that they were easy to open and opened outwards.

(*The Graphic, June 23rd, 1883; The London Times June 18th, July 3rd, July 5th, 1883*)

Plague and Pestilence

Some people don't fear death, but they do fear how they'll die. Centuries ago when medicine was in its infancy in terms of germs, diagnosis and treatment, a sickness that appeared from nowhere, killed vast numbers, disappeared and resurfaced years later, had to be feared. The Black Death or plague was such a sickness and when it occurred in 1348-9 it decimated 50% of our population!

Today we usually associate the plague with London in the Middle Ages, but the north didn't escape. For instance the population in six hamlets around Belford was so decimated that the cemetery had to be enlarged; 78% of Jarrow Priory's tenants died and County Durham had a 60% mortality rate.

It's thought the plague was spread from China across Europe by ships carrying rats laden with bacteria carrying fleas and killed 75 million people across the world.

However, a new theory has been put forward by contemporary historians such as Dr. B. Sloane which questions this. He reasons that there would have been a decrease in rats and fleas in the winter of 1348 as the cold would have killed them. Though rats can be killed by bubonic plague, no one has found large heaps of 14th century rat bones. He also states that it spread too quickly for it to be rats. He argues it was spread by person to person contact in, *'crowded medieval cities'*. He is even doubtful that it was bubonic plague.

Well, until the scientists find the definitive answer, let's stick to what we believe to be correct. In the past plague was blamed on the usual scapegoats: sin, Jews poisoning wells (impossible as Jews were expelled by Edward I in 1290) and evil humours in the air. The suggested cures: avoid lechery and fruit, but drink good wine.

St. Nicholas' Cathedral, Newcastle. A plague pit containing over 300 bodies, lies beneath Queen Victoria's statue which stands outside.

You probably know of two types of plague pneumonic and bubonic, but did you know there was a third, septicemic? The viral strains Yersinia pestis, Xenopsylla cheopsis or Cortophylus fasciatus appear to have caused the plague. It could survive for up to 6 months in cargo bales or dung heaps, all in plentiful supply in the medieval world. It wasn't usually a problem, but for reasons we don't yet understand, at times there was an increase in the bacilli in the flea's stomach. This caused a blockage which was regurgitated when the flea bit a victim. The plague was then passed to them.

Pneumonic plague could be spread to others and was a severe type of lung infection. It was rare, but more deadly than the other types of plague as 95-100% of its victims died within three days! It was caused by inhaling infected droplets. The symptoms were: a headache, a fever, chest pain, a cough, red blood or water in sputum, weakness, shortness of breath followed rapidly by pneumonia. Secondary pneumonic plague formed after the bubonic and septicemic plagues lay untreated when the disease was in the lungs.

Bubonic plague was thought to have been caused by rat or flea bites or more rarely the bacilli could enter the body, possibly from infected clothing through a cut in the skin. Until we have a scientific answer, it's the only explanation that seems to be out there. It affected the lymphatic system (a major part of the immune system). The symptoms were severe headaches, high fever, vomit, black spots, purple blotches, coughing up blood, diarrhoea, large buboes (tender lymph glands sometimes

A doctor's protective clothing during plague.

as large as apples) filled with blood and pus appeared in armpits and between legs, respiratory failure and others. Lastly when attacking the nervous system it created problems with the nerves, brain, spinal cord and finally the mind linked to the danse macabre (a medieval dance where death is represented by a skeleton leading others to the grave). The good news? Bubonic plague only killed 50-60% of its victims.

Septicemic plague was contracted in a similar way to bubonic and occurred when the blood stream was infected. If pneumonic and bubonic plague were left untreated septicemic plague could appear as a complication of this. The symptoms were: a rash within hours, chills, fever, abdominal pain, weakness, bleeding beneath the skin and shock, but no buboes. Though rare, unfortunately it was always fatal and killed within a day! (*Daily Mail, Friday, August 19th, 2011, p.20*)

This is what happened in the North East in the 16th and 17th centuries.

1587 – A Plague on All the Houses
Hartlepool and Hart

There were 26 deaths deaths in Hartlepool, double the usual number. (*Sykes, Vol.1, p.79*)

On May 21st a record states, '*here began the sickness.*' There were 89 corpses buried at Hart, one young, unknown woman died in the street. (*Stranton Register, County Durham*)

Newcastle

In 1588 and 1589 the plague came to Newcastle and killed 1,727 people. In Newcastle in, '*August, 1589, Edward Errington, the towne's foole, buried the 23d August, died in the peste.*' (*St. John's Register, Newcastle*)

The plague also struck Durham in 1589. Many of the poor who survived, removed themselves to live in huts and sheds on the commons, such as Elvet Moor and Bishop Matthew retreated to his Stockton castle.

Durham and County Durham

On May 21st, 1597: '*Heere began the sickness*' (the plague). Ninety-three people died in 1597. Amongst the victims were: '*Raphe Turner ye vicar, July 27; Richard Turner, brother to ye sad Raphe, buried the same day.*' (*Parochial Register Vol. 1, Stranton, County Durham*)

In July 1597 the plague devastated Auckland, Aycliffe, Billingham, Boldon, Burdon, Chester-le-Street, Durham, Darlington, Gateshead, Houghton, Stainton, St. Helen, Whickham, Wolsingham and a number of other places.

As the plague raged in 1597 the list of the dead grew:

DATE	PLACE	DEATHS
October 17th	Darlington	340
October 27th	Elvet, in the city of Durham	400 +
	St. Nicholas' parish	100
	St. Margaret's parish	200
	St. Giles' parish	60
	St. Mary's in the North Bailey	60
	The gaol	24
July 11th - November 27th	St. Nicholas' parish, Durham	215

A number of plague victims were buried in St. Thomas' chapel, beyond Claypath or on the moor.

At the beginning of 1598 the plague stopped claiming victims in Darlington and Durham, but began again *'on September 15'*.

In 1604 there were plague victims in St. Giles' parish in the city of Durham. People who had died of the plague in Newcastle were noted in St. Nicholas' register in 1609 and 78 deaths of, *'the pestilence'* were recorded in July 1610 in the parish register of Lamsley, in County Durham.

The plague raged again in Gateshead and Newcastle in 1623 and in October 1635 the plague arrived at North Shields. By 1636 it was back in Newcastle and from May 6th to December 31st, 5,307 people died. There was no trade and roads were deserted. Between May 30th and October 17th of the same year, 515 people also died of the plague in Gateshead

There were some positives. The poor who survived the plague found themselves in a better bargaining position with their masters. There were vast tracts of land with no apparent owner, many probably took advantage of this. A shortage of labour meant peasants were paid more. (*Sykes, Vol. 1, p.82*)

However, plague wasn't the only disease to strike down the population, Cholera arrived in the early 19th century.

Cholera

Cholera is an infection of the small intestine, a form of gastroenteritis caused by a toxin produced by the bacterium vibrio cholerae which can be found in brackish water and estuaries. If it enters the water supply an outbreak of cholera can occur. It's rare in countries where quality of water is monitored and drainage is good, but it can spread quickly if water is tainted and there's poor sanitation

By the 20th century the world had experienced six major cholera pandemics. In the 19th century epidemics in Great Britain occurred in 1831, 1848, 1853 and 1866.

Cholera was first described in Jassur, India when noticed among British troops. It was in Russia by 1823 and Hamburg in 1831. The government of Great Britain instructed that all ships arriving from the Baltic ports should be put under quarantine in January 1831.

Unfortunately, the authorities in Sunderland, appeared to know better. Despite the fact that there was no regulation of water, sanitation or housing, there was no quarantine of ships in Sunderland harbour. In October, 1831, a ship carrying sick sailors was allowed to dock. Their symptoms would have been profuse diarrhoea; painful retching; thirst and dehydration; severe pain in abdominal muscles, stomach, limbs and occasionally a bluish-grey skin.

Death arrives by coach in Sunderland. This was a print produced during the time when the town was under quarantine. It illustrates the double standards that while there were restrictions on ships coming in and out of Sunderland, road traffic continued.

The young and elderly were particularly vulnerable. The first case in Sunderland was possibly, river pilot, Robert Henry, but the nature of his death was unreported. Next, 12 year old, Isabella Hazard, who lived near the quayside became ill and died inside 24 hours. The third death was that of William Sproat, a 60 year old keelman, who lived close to Isabella. Dr. James Butler Kell was called and he realised it was cholera having witnessed and contained it in Mauritius some years before.

Kell requested the assistance of Dr. William Reid Clanny, Head of the Board of Health's medical department in Sunderland. Meanwhile, Sproat survived for three days, but when he died, he was named as the first 'official' victim of cholera. The next to die were Sproat's son, granddaughter and nurse. The authorities still hadn't been notified four days later, so Kell did this and forced Clanny to act.

All ships now had to stay under quarantine in harbour for 15 days. Unbelievably, local businessmen, worried about losing profits, formed an anti-cholera party to discredit the idea that cholera was to blame. What is worse, an extraordinary meeting of the board was called but, Kell and Clanny refused to attend. One after another, Sunderland's doctors withdrew their former claims that cholera was in Sunderland! The nation was scandalised. Were the doctors influenced by the businessmen?

With the death toll rising, Sunderland's surviving cholera victims, frightened of post mortems and possible body snatching refused to go to cholera hospitals. Jarrow, in County Durham even created a floating cholera hospital at Jarrow Slake, close to St. Paul's Monastery.

Kell and Clanny, to their credit, gave blankets to the poor and, concerned about unsanitary conditions, provided quicklime and men who cleaned the streets twice a day. Their sanitising campaign attracted doctors from across the globe to visit Sunderland.

By late December, Sunderland's cholera epidemic, after 215 deaths, seemed to be over, but Gateshead received its first victims at Christmas followed shortly by Newcastle. By the time it had spread to the whole country, cholera had killed 32,000 people. It must have been terrifying.

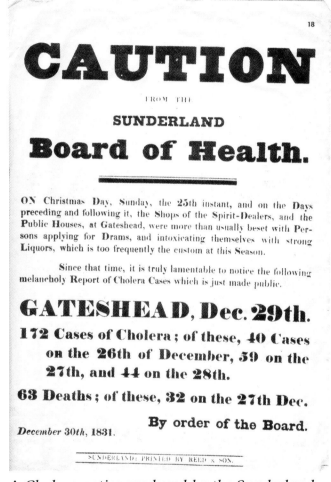

A *Cholera notice produced by the Sunderland Board of Health.*

On January 9th, 1832, the Board of Health declared Sunderland free of cholera.

Meanwhile in a small Tyneside colliery at Killingworth, another doctor, John Snow working with cholera victims made an important discovery. Though he was to die years later without recognition, he was the first to disprove two popular theories at the time: one that cholera was spread by contagion and victims should be isolated and the miasma theory that it was caused by bad smells, or bad air, most doctors didn't think beyond those two. Snow discovered that cholera was a water-borne disease and he did eventually share his knowledge in the London cholera epidemic in 1848.

Financial Disaster
Beastly Banks!

Everyone thought banks were secure, after all there hadn't been a 'run' on a bank in England since the London wholesale discount bank of Overend and Gurney in 1866. In 2007 Northern Rock plc became the first English bank to experience a 'run' in modern times. Who could forget the queues of depositors wanting to withdraw their savings or that in 2008 the bank was taken into public ownership and subsequently bought by Virgin Money?

However, Northern Rock plc was not the first bank in Newcastle to experience a 'run'. Notes were first issued from the Newcastle Bank established in August 22nd, 1755. On December 1st, 1755 notice was given, *'that the Newcastle bank founded by Robert Carr, a merchant who traded with the Baltic, would be opened on this day,'* at the house of Mr. Robinson's in Pilgrim Street, where all business in the banking and the exchange would be transacted as in London.

Several provincial banks came into being in the early 1790s. For instance the Newcastle banks in 1793 were: The Old Bank (which became Ridley, Cookson, & Co.); the Exchange (which became Surtees, Burdon, & Co.); the Tyne (which became Baker, Hedley, & Co.); the Commercial (which became Forster, Burrell, Rankin, & Co.) and The Bank (which became R. J. Lambton & Co.).

However, from 1789-1799 France was in the throes of a revolution. On January 21st, 1793 King Louis XVI of France was executed. France, once a feudal state with a king, became a republic with an empire under Napoleon Bonaparte. These events precipitated a series of European wars which raged for twenty-three years from 1792-

A humourous postcard produced after a crashed vehicle almost demolished a bank in Gateshead.

1815. The wars were unpopular in Britain and paid for by income tax, so households had little money to spare.

On February 19th, 1793 the Bank of England, *'refused the paper of Lane, Son, and Fraser ...'* who were, *'deep in corn speculation'* and they failed for a million the next day. Could the banks be trusted? There was panic in London, though a letter from Newcastle's Lambton & Co. stated, *'... we in the north remain undisturbed and quiet here.'*

A month later the panic had spread to the rest of the country including Newcastle. Numerous London banks failed, many who acted for those in the north. Alarm was spread by the appointment of New London agents, *'advertised in local papers ...'* People across the country wanted gold, not a paper note in their hands. And who could blame them?

London was inundated by provincial bankers demanding gold and trying to get it home. Mr. Rowland Bardon, a partner in Newcastle's Exchange Bank, was no exception. He'd got his gold and was heading north in his post chaise when he was held up by footpads. He was fortunate, as they emptied his pockets, they didn't notice the gold.

Things became desperate in Newcastle. The banks managed to meet their customers' demands from Monday April 1st to Saturday April 6th until the Commercial *'could hold out no longer.'* So on Monday April 8th, the banks decided to, *'suspend payments for some time.'*

On the same day in an effort to still the panic, the mayor, James Rudman, Esq. held a public meeting in support of the banks. The members of the meeting resolved, *'That the Banks of Ridley, Cookson, and Company; Surtees, Burdon, and Company; Baker, Hedley, and Company; of this town are Banks of unquestionable Credit, and are entitled to the Confidence of the Public in the fullest Extent.'* On April 10th, tradesmen in Gateshead followed suit. Newcastle banks were back to business as usual, six weeks after the failure of Lane, Son and Fraser.

A £1 note printed in 1803 by the Surtees, Burdon and Brandling Bank in Newcastle.

One source points out that, *'The subscribed capital of the bankers in the north was insignificant, and we may assume deposits under the same term, as the lives of the bank were very short.'* Worryingly the northern banks appeared to have relied on the confidence of customers in the bank as opposed to having an amount of capital which would cover all contingencies.

In 1795 the country was still engaged in an expensive war with France. There was always the fear of invasion and the Northumberland coast became one long army camp. The situation was obviously unstable leading to another 'run' on the banks in 1795:

Saturday February 18th, 1795

'the rapid and enormous increase of the national debt, and the alarm of the invasion (by the French) caused a run upon the provincial banking houses. The proprietors of the Newcastle banks agreed ... to suspend their payments early on Monday morning for a short time.' (Mackenzie 1827)

In 1797, invasion became reality when the French landed in Wales. The government demanded, *'livestock, carts, and defensive instruments'* from farmers near the east coast as well as an inventory of their stock which was to *'... be driven into the interior ...'* Alarmed farmers drove carts full of grain to Newcastle, *'... and sold it for any price they could get ...'* As they were paid in notes, they sped to the banks demanding specie (coin as opposed to paper money).

The banks were forced to take action and stated on Saturday February 18th that, *'if the demand for gold was so great on Monday morning they'd suspend payment till more specie could be obtained.'* (Philips, J. 1894, A History of Banks ...)

Section Three – Dastardly Deeds

Dastardly deeds reflect some of the more negative aspects of human nature.

A peaceful Hexham Market Place in 1810. Fifty years previously, the Market Place was the setting for a riot!

Riots

Riots in modern Britain? Occurring in city after city on the same day? Unthinkable! Or so we thought until August 2011 when rioting started in London and spread to Birmingham, Liverpool, Nottingham, Bristol and Manchester.

In 1066 William of Normandy conquered England, or so he thought. He hadn't reckoned with those in the north ...

1069 – Revolting Peasants

An incident in Durham concerning Robert Cumwyn, Earl of Northumberland, caused William the Conqueror to turn the sixty miles from York to Durham into a wasteland by burning crops and slaughtering the inhabitants.

Quartered in Durham with 700 Norman soldiers, Cumwyn had enforced the Conqueror's authority by cruelly oppressing those opposed to Norman rule, but the murder of several landowners instigated a riot by peasants who broke open the city gates at dawn and slaughtered the Normans. A number of soldiers barricaded themselves in the Cumyn's lodgings. This was set on fire and the cathedral's western tower caught alight. The cathedral was only saved by the wind changing direction. Cumwyn and all but one of his 700 men died!

Durham and the River Wear.

William the Conqueror wasn't best pleased again in 1080 when a mob killed a Bishop and his guards.

1080 – The Murderous Mob and the Normans' Revenge

A popular Saxon nobleman called Liulph and his family were murdered. Unpopular, Walcher, Bishop of Durham, who'd purchased the Earldom of Northumberland, didn't apprehend Liulph's murderers. The Bishop held a public assembly in Gateshead and a mob appeared. The Bishop, frightened for his life, used his officers to assure the mob that restitution would be given to the deceased Liulph's relatives.

Shouting that they were going to slay the Bishop, the protestors drew concealed weapons from their clothing and killed his guards. The Bishop fled to the church and sent men out to appease the crowd, but a number were slain. They then set the church alight and killed anyone fleeing the flames. The last to come out was the Bishop, saying a prayer and covering his face. A lance was thrust into his heart and the mob then attacked his body with swords. Marching to Durham, they tried to take the castle, but after holding the city for four days, they fled the vengeance to come.

Retribution

William the Conqueror was furious and sent his brother Odo, Bishop of Bayeux, to find the murderers. Odo performed his task like a Norman soldier. He killed the rebels' innocent relatives; stole a rich staff from the church of Durham and pretended it had been taken by soldiers and then laid waste to the north. Odo didn't have the support of a Riot Act.

The Riot Act, passed in 1714, formally, 'An Act for preventing tumults and riotous assemblies, and for the more speedy and effectual punishing the rioters' came into being in 1715 because of concerns about attempts to overthrow George I by Jacobite mobs. There were rebellions in Scotland in 1715 and 1745, so their fears were well founded.

However, the Riot Act gave the government sweeping powers. Any group of twelve or more who gave the authorities cause for concern could be noted as a 'riotous and tumultuous assembly' and read the Riot Act by a magistrate.

If the group hadn't disbanded within an hour, they could have been arrested and given a sentence of up to two years hard labour or not less than three years penal servitude. It wasn't until 1973 that the Riot Act was repealed and in 1986 the Public Order Act superseded it.

In 1761, the people of Hexham were read the Riot Act.

Durham Castle was built in 1072 by order of William the Conqueror. The keep was constructed in the 14th century and rebuilt in the 1840s.

March 9th, 1761 – Hell in Hexham!

Feelings ran high in Hexhamshire. Like the rest of northern England, Hexhamshire didn't want a system of balloting for the militia in which parishes listed all adult males and ballots were held where individuals were chosen for compulsory military service.

In February, 1761 A mob of a thousand arrived in Gateshead with a petition in an attempt to stop the ballot and delivered it to the Deputy-Lieutenants. It said:

Durham, February 27th, 1761
'... it is far from the hearts of any of us that is here met today to be in anyways inclined to be rebellious against his Royal Majesty; but, far from it, only what common men desire is men of estates to hire men for the militia as they were formerly; being very fit that they who have lands should hire men to maintain them; for it is a thing that none

of us will submit to, to be allotted after this manner, as it is vain to enlist or draw any belonging to this our country: for we are resolved not to let any man go out amongst us in this manner.

God save his Majesty King George the Third'

To avoid inflaming the situation the Deputy-Lieutenants excused the petitioners at their expense, apart from *'a trifle ... on whom the lots fell.'* Only about twelve men were required from the ward.

By March a large number of people in Northumberland appeared to assume that those in Durham had been exempted from the ballot.

In Morpeth a mob tore or burnt all the lists and books in front of the constables. They acted in the same way in Whittingham a day later.

Flushed with their success, the mob numbered 5,000 when they arrived at Hexham on March 9th where there was to be a ballot for men in the Tindale (Tynedale) ward. The local magistrates had already been warned there might be a riot and ensured that two battalions of the North Yorkshire Militia, quartered in Newcastle, were in Hexham and drawn up in ranks in front of the Moot Hall.

The clock tower in Morpeth was built using medieval stone between 1604 and 1634.

The sight of the soldiers infuriated the mob. Petitions were presented and the ringleaders argued for four hours with the magistrates until the Riot Act was read. It warned:

'Our sovereign Lord the King chargeth and commandeth all persons assembled, immediately to disperse themselves, and peaceably to depart to their habitations, or to their lawful business, upon the pains contained in the act made in the first year of King George, for preventing tumults and riotous assemblies. God save the King.'

The Riot Act 1715.

The soldiers had bayonets at the ready. The mob held staves, clubs and quarter staffs. According to William Allen, an officer in the North Yorks Militia, a firelock belonging to a soldier in Captain Blomberg's company was seized. It was used to shoot the soldier. Then a pistol was used to kill Ensign Hart. Panic ensued and the magistrates gave out the order for general fire. Lancelot Allgood, the

Hexham Market Place in 1820.

Deputy-Lieutenant, appears to be the most likely candidate for ordering the soldiers to shoot.

The mob scattered leaving the square empty apart from the severely wounded and the dead. It's thought 300 were wounded and 45 died. However, many fled and may have died or recovered in their own homes, any participation in the riot unacknowledged for fear of prosecution. The surviving rioters were hunted for several weeks and it is popularly thought that Allgood and Christopher Reed from Chipchase hid from the rioters in a hay loft on the Hexham Road.

Allen records that the men who instigated the riot by killing the soldiers were themselves, *'instantly despatched'*, also that Colonel Dunscombe's detachment had a mortally wounded officer, one dead private and three wounded.

On August 17th, two men, Peter Patterson and William Elder were convicted of treason and sentenced:

'To be drawn upon a hurdle to the place of execution on Wednesday, the 30th day of September next, and then and there severally hanged by the neck, to be cut down alive, and have their entrails taken out and burnt before their faces, to have their heads severed from their bodies and their bodies severally divided into four quarters and their breads and quarters disposed of at his majesty's pleasure.'

However, not all sentences go to plan and the executions were postponed until October 5th when Peter Patterson, was drawn and then hanged, according to the first two parts of his sentence in Morpeth.

Unbelievably the noose gave way and he fell! Patterson was supposed to have said, *'Innocent blood is ill shed.'* Then he had to be hanged all over again, and finally quartered. Fortunately, William Elder was pardoned in August, 1762.
(*Sykes, Vol.1, p.231-234*)

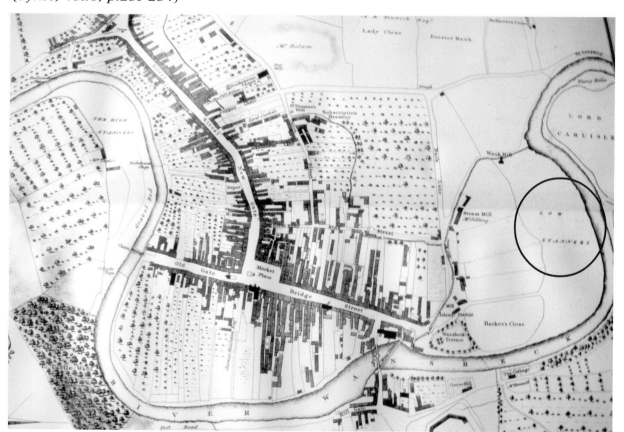

Morpeth with Low Stanners (circled), on the right in the bend of the River Wansbeck. Executions were carried out here. Map dated 1826.

Apart from reluctant recruits for the militia, the ordinary person also had other reasons to riot. Injustice, poverty, unemployment and famine all had their part to play and governments have always been fearful of the mob. A starving mob must have been a terrifying sight.

Famine Riots

1315-1317 were the years of the Great Famine in Northern Europe. Crop failures on a grand scale were responsible. Hunger and want caused crime levels to rise, mass death, disease, infanticide and even cannibalism.

1317 – Cannibalism in Newcastle

There were many deaths caused by a famine in Newcastle. It is reported that some of the inhabitants *'eat the flesh of their own children, and thieves in prison devoured those that were brought in, and greedily eat them half alive.'*
(*Sykes, Vol.1, p.36*)

In June, 1740 Corn was scarce and therefore the price went up again in Newcastle and the people rioted.

The Guildhall Riot in Newcastle

The militia was raised and the mob disbanded when promised that corn would be cheaper in the future. The following day Alderman Ridley accompanied by the militia (mostly young apprentices who wore white stockings and became known as The White Stocking Regiment) informed the people that the corn-factors had set the price on their grain. Rye would be sold at 5s, wheat at 7s and meslin (a type of flour) at 5s 6d per boll. The crowd declared themselves satisfied at that.

However, on the June 21st, when a number of keelmen, pitmen and the poor, tried to buy corn at the price they'd been promised, they found the factors had shut their shops and that most had fled. The granaries were then plundered by the mob. In the following days when a vessel was seen to be leaving with a quantity of rye, it was stopped and some sold to the poor at the previously agreed price. The militia was disbanded on the 25th perhaps giving the people a false sense of power. On the following day, the mayor, a number of aldermen and some other gentlemen met at the Guidhall to discuss what to do next. At the same time a huge crowd gathered nearby in the market place at Sandhill and became more and more threatening. On hearing a gentlemen tell them that a ship at the quay would supply the poor with rye, the mob knocked him down and wounded him.

Re-assembling, the militia opened fire, killing one rioter and seriously wounding several others. Incensed, the mob turned on the gentlemen in the Guildhall wounding most of them and left a trail of destruction throughout Newcastle. They destroyed woodwork, tore two paintings of Charles II and James II, leaving only their faces; broke windows; ransacked the town court and chamber; destroyed public accounts and writings; stole money from the corporation and when finding shops closed, roamed the streets threatening to destroy and burn Newcastle!

Newcastle in the 1800s.

Captain Sowle, commanding three companies of Howard's regiment, marched his men from Alnwick and entered Newcastle. The mob dispersed and forty rioters were flung in prison. Thomas Grey, James Harriot, Robert Hatherick (alias Hatherwick), William Keed (alias Kid or Keedy), William Sopit, Jacob Trotter and Thomas Wilson were convicted at the assizes and sentenced to transportation for seven years.

The people were poor, starving and desperate. On June 14th, 1740 a multitude gathered in Durham and offered farmers 8s per boll for wheat. This was refused. The corn was seized and a fight broke out. On June 20th in Sunderland the mob grabbed a great quantity of wheat so they could sell it for 4s a bushel.

The harvest failed again in 1800 and war with France didn't help the economy. At least soup kitchens were set up, though some of the public appeared to be mean spirited.

January 4th, 1800

'The bad harvest ... and the effects of war, combined to produce such a dearth, that wheat in Newcastle market sold at one guinea a Winchester bushel ... a public meeting was held in the Guildhall, Newcastle, for the purpose of establishing a public soup-kitchen for the relief of the poor, and to which benevolent scheme the corporation gave 50 guineas. At this period of suffering and ill humour, the public viewed all those who trafficked in the necessaries of life with an evil eye; and on August 18th, a meeting was held to devise punishment all for forestallers and regraters!' (Mackenzie, 1827)

Keelmen rioted because they were losing work.

Rebellions of the Belly

Newcastle keelmen were amongst the best paid workers at the time. Nevertheless there were strikes in 1709, 1710 and 1750 called, *'rebellions of the belly'* but only because the keelmen were prepared to strike almost to the point of starvation. In an attempt to break a strike, keelmen were *'press ganged'* into the Navy in 1719.

There were no warnings in the 19th century when there was a strike in 1819; it began on September 27th when they prevented keels navigating on the Tyne. The keelmen issued a petition to the owners and fitters on September 28th. They complained that below the bridge, the spouts (chutes) were taking employment from the keelmen; they wanted colliers to load 6 keels of coal and return to the mouth of the river so the keels would load the rest. They also wanted a maximum of eight Newcastle chauldrons to fill a keel and this to be strictly adhered to.

When the weight of coals was exceeded, the keels became even more difficult

'Tyne Colliers' with kind permission of the artist, Malcolm Teasdale.

to handle and in bad weather or with a strong tide, could capsize. Their last concern was about funding for the Keelman's Hospital.

In the past each keelman paid a 1d a chauldron into the hospital fund, but the coal from the chauldrons which deposited coal directly into colliers, bypassed the keelmen and the fund was losing money.

The coalowners called a General Meeting on October 2nd where they agreed to contribute £300 to the Keelmen's Hospital Fund and to restrict the amount of coal per chauldron. However, they refused to interfere with the workings of the spout.

The riot took place on October 14th, 1819 in North Shields and the mayor believed the men came from a village three miles away.

According to a letter written by the Mayor of Newcastle to Lord Sidmouth on October 17th, 1819, possibly 700 men (mainly forgemen) carried concealed weapons.

North Shields in 1830.

Keelmen had stopped wagons and committed other acts of lawlessness. The magistrates accompanied by dragoons agreed to go down both banks of the Tyne, whilst the mayor went on the river. Three miles from Shields, four ships from the Royal Navy met the mayor.

Ships loaded coal and a steam packet remained behind guarding the keel's crew and the mayor went ashore.

Within 20 minutes the packet was under attack and requested help from the mayor. He borrowed Captain Montague's boats but was prevented from reaching the packet by a mob of three to four hundred standing pelting stones from the quay. Within minutes the Royal Navy arrived, but was beaten back. The mayor managed to capture an apparent leader, a shoemaker, whilst he was bending to throw stones. The shoemaker had employed several workmen and had marched from Shields on the 11th. After a few minutes there was the sound of two muskets fired in the air by marines, more shots followed and Joseph Cleckson was killed.

The furious mob blamed the mayor who was sheltering in a house owned by the Duke of Northumberland. Magistrates from Shields were requested, but had been unable to get there. The house was surrounded by the mob and the room the mayor was in was attacked with brickbats and stones and windows were destroyed.

The mayor went to the door to explain that the man's death was not his fault, but was driven back by a hail of stones, two of which hit him! Just as the mob broke in, the High Constable, Mr. Joshua Donkin arrived and assured the rioters that the mayor couldn't have given the order to fire. The mob demanded the shoemaker and he was given to them, but the violence began again and within minutes the mob rushed through the front door suspecting the mayor was hiding there. They searched every room and even looked in chests for him. Meanwhile, the mayor and Mr. Donkin made a speedy exit out of the back door and unrecognized got away.

The mayor sent to Lord Darlington for four companies of the 40th who arrived at four on Friday morning and more were due the following day. He reported a state of near rebellion, the motive being a dispute between the owners and keelmen.

The keelmen finally agreed to the coalowners' offer of: £300 for their hospital fund; an Act of Parliament that ensured the collection of one farthing per chauldron of coal shipped from the Tyne by keel or collier; backdated pay for the amount of coal above eight Newcastle chauldrons carried by a keel; the Inspector of Staithes being responsible for the eight chauldron limit; a copy of their annual bond; 2s 6d for a keel loaded by hand; ships' captains paying 1 shilling per keel for every foot the coalport was above the gunwhale (the top); £1 to be paid at '*Binding time*' to assist with housing rents and Newcastle Corporation hiring unemployed keelmen to dredge the Tyne. The keelmen returned to work on October 22nd; the strike had only lasted 22 days.

This wasn't the end of the keelmens' grievances. Three years later there was another strike.

October 24th, 1822 – Keelmen Strike

'*... during a strike by the keelmen of the Tyne, a number of seamen proceeded to force the crews from some vessels loading at the spouts. The mayor of Newcastle, Robert Bell Esq. immediately proceeded down the river in his barge, with an army of volunteers and police, and took 32 rioters into custody, who after being guarded all night in a king's cutter, were next brought to the Castle of Newcastle. A number of seamen accompanied their captured companions; and in the Castle Garth, their conduct was so turbulent, that the riot act was read. Thus the intended strike of keelmen was frustrated at the commencement. The keelmen after a suspension of ten weeks, resumed their labour at the beginning of December.*' (Mackenzie, 1827)

Soldiers man the boats during the keelmen's strike on the Tyne at Newcastle in 1822.

Concerns about continued employment and fair pay for an honest day's work weren't the only reasons for rioting. Some heady wine, lots of frothy beer and a huge feast and you have a potent mix when celebrating the coronation of a king in 1821.

July 19th, 1821 – Coronation Riot

'... the coronation of his majesty George IV was celebrated in Newcastle. An elegant pant 12 foot high was erected in the centre of Sandhill. When the magistrates returned and appeared at the great window of the Town's Court to drink his majesty's health, which was accompanied by a royal salute from the Castle, the wine began to flow from the

pant. An indescribable scene of the most indecent uproar ensued; and one man clung to the top of the erection until all his clothes were torn from his body. When the wine ceased to flow, the pant was torn to pieces, and the mob began to throw about the pots, soaked hats, caps ... Galleries were erected on the tops of some houses, to witness the disgusting spectacle. In the meadows, an ox, that had been roasted at the bottom of the Old Flesh Market, was hoisted upon the platform, and cut into pieces, which were thrown among the crowd. This insulting mode of distribution was promptly resented, and the persons on the stage were pelted with the pieces of meat and bones. The remains of the animal were then dragged by the chain of the crane, through the streets of Sandhill; the furnace was pulled down; the procession of mail coaches passing at the time was wantonly assailed with brickbats ... The ale-pant in the Old Flesh Market was demolished while the beer was still running. The Spital pant was also pulled down ... About three o'clock, the multitude was attracted to the Moor, to witness the race, which tended to preserve the peace of the town. At night, the

A 19th century pant.

police succeeded in depressing the disorderly crowds that continued to demolish the temporary erections in the Spital and the Old Flesh Market.' (*Mackenzie, 1827*)

War

War has always been with us, but perhaps the border regions of the United Kingdom have suffered the most and the north in particular. Not only did we have to suffer invasions by Danes, Romans and Normans, but the Scots frequently crossed the border and did battle; there were raids, rebellions and then reivers and mosstroopers made life almost impossible for any who dared to survive.

The Scots

King Canute of England regarded the Lothian area of Scotland as his by right. He ignored a blazing comet which foretold the Northumbrian's defeat and sent Huctred, Earl of Northumberland and his Angle army to try to regain it. Huctred's force was massacred on the banks of the Tweed at the Battle of Carham in 1018 by Malcolm II, King of Alba, leader of the joint Briton and Scots forces

The Church of Scotland

From the mid 16th century, Presbyterianism was a branch of the reformed church in Scotland and governed by lay elders of equal rank and local assemblies of clergy. The church had been reformed by John Knox's interpretation of Calvinism and later Andrew Melville and his Presbyterian system of church government.

It meant that in 1618 the General Assembly of the Scottish church reluctantly agreed to accept the Five Articles of Perth. This was James I's attempt to integrate Episcopacy (Popish church government) into the Kirk.

In 1638, Charles I also tried to replace the Presbyterian structure with Episcopalian (high Anglican) church government. This meant the church being led by a 'popish' hierarchy of bishops. Charles I's interference wasn't welcomed by the Scottish church and resulted in the signing of the Scottish National Covenant.

The Covenanters united opposition to the reforms and were the prime religious and political group in Scotland. With the Covenanters and King at loggerheads and neither willing to give way, military action was perhaps inevitable and culminated in the Bishops' War of 1639-1640.

The First Bishops' War

The Lords of Argyll, Balmerino, Montrose and Rothes were Covenanters and prepared for war, even appealing to absent Scots to come and fight on their side.

Charles I raised an army of 20,000 and put the Marquis of Hamilton in charge of the navy. But the English Puritans sympathised with the Covenanters; Charles I was short of funds and there was little enthusiasm for war. After being driven back by the Scots, Charles I said he'd address the Scots' grievances once order was restored and as long as the Scots stayed 10 miles north of the border and didn't invade.

There were rumours the Scots had overwhelming numbers compared to the English. After negotiations, the Covenanters signed the Pacification of Berwick in June 1639. But it wasn't over. Neither side trusted the other and Charles I returned to London in July determined to beat the Covenanters. So it comes as no surprise that there was a Second Bishops' War and a battle in Northumberland.

The Second Bishops' War
August 20th, 1640 – The Battle of Newburn

Scots Covenanters, under General David Leslie invaded England by fording the Tweed and marching to Newburn, four miles from Newcastle where they were met by Lord Conway commander of the English forces guarding the ford over the Tyne.

The Scots pitched their tents on Heddon Law, above Newburn. They placed their cannon in Newburn Church's steeple and ensured the lanes and hedges around the village were lined with musketry.

An illustration of Newburn-on-Tyne showing the commanding position the church had over the surrounding area.

The English army, consisting of about 300 foot and 1,500 horse were on Stella Haugh, a meadow south of the Tyne. They'd strengthened their position by having cannon, musketry and throwing up two breast works.

The start of the battle was triggered by a Scot's officer wearing a black feather in his hat, leaving a thatched house in Newburn to water his horse. An English officer felt that the Scot was spying on trenches which were south of the Tyne. He shot the Scot!

The Scots had the advantage of position, numbers and discipline and once an ebb tide made the river fordable, their cannon had driven the English back. A forlorn hope of 26 horse under Major Ballantyne dug in on the south bank. However, with Scots fording the river in great numbers, the English retreated in a disorderly manner which became a rout and Northumberland, Durham and Newcastle, with its royal stores and magazines lay open to the Scots. There was no one on the streets of Newcastle, fearing the Scots would give no quarter. Not one of 400 ships dared to tie up at the Quayside as shops were shut and homes were deserted. The Scots paid for cheese, bread and corn with money or a promissory note, but if the offer was refused, they took what they wanted.

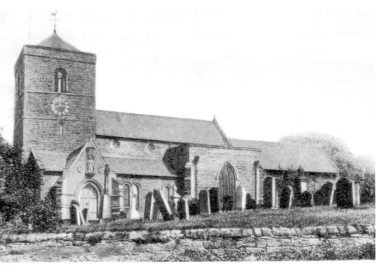

Newburn Church where the Scottish forces sited their cannon in 1640.

Saddler Street – one of Durham's ancient streets.

Durham

There was panic in Durham and the people fled in droves. One in ten houses was vacant; no shop was open for four days after the fight and there was no food or drink because the king's army had '*visited*' on their way south. The Bishop of Durham fled to his castle in Stockton.

By August 30th, the Scots arrived at Durham. The counties of Northumberland and Durham were told to pay levies of £350 and £300 respectively per day, besides giving them '*hay and stray*'. The Scots, having received £60,000, left the area.

Commonwealth Capers

When Charles I was executed, Oliver Cromwell was sent to Ireland and Scotland to suppress the Royalists. On July 15th, 1650, he entered Newcastle with his army on the way to Scotland. He was feted with fine food and drink, followed by a fast to ensure God was on his side. Five Newcastle regiments joined his 16,000 man army. After winning the Battle of Dunbar, Cromwell arrived in Newcastle and recommended that the Scottish prisoners were treated with humanity. A large number were marched south to Newcastle and Sir Arthur Haslerigg's letter to the Council of State, revealed what actually happened to some of them:

October 31st, 1650 – Newcastle

'*When they came to Morpeth, the prisoners being put into a large garden, they eat up raw cabbages, leaves and roots, so many as the very seed and labour, at 4d a day, was valued at 9d, which cabbage (they having fasted, as they themselves said, near eight days) poisoned their bodies, for as they were coming hence to Newcastle, some died by the way-side: when they came to Newcastle I put them in the greatest church in the town, and the next morning when I sent them off to Durham, about 140 were sick and not able to march – three died that night, and some fell down in their march from Newcastle to Durham, and died. On being told into the great cathedral church, they were counted to be no more than 3,000, although Col. Fenwick wrote me there were about 3,500 ...*' (Sykes, Vol. 1 p.106)

The survivors were transported to colonies like the West Indies and New England.

Raids

Sudden military attacks were common. Danish raids came from the sea and local rivers were their highway. There were numerous raids along the Northumberland coast.

The Danes' first raid on England was in 789 AD and four years later they set fire to and pillaged Lindisfarne's monastery. Those who didn't flee were butchered. Returning a year later, the Danes raided the monastery at Jarrow, though this time Offa, King of Mercia, their leader was killed when they were defeated by Northumbrian forces.

The survivors of the battle set off in their ships, but were shipwrecked off Tynemouth.

Later in 800 AD, both Hartlepool and Tynemouth

Lindisfarne causeway, illustrating the island's isolation.

monasteries were raided by the Danes and 32 years after this there was a report of an attempted landing at Tynemouth by Danish pirates, but they were repelled and fled to their ships.

Watercolour of St. Paul's Monastery, Jarrow. Artist unknown.

Tynemouth monastery was destroyed by Danes in 866 AD and nine years later they appeared even more fearless.

Halfden, a Dane, arrived with several ships and sailed up the Tyne. They wintered in local villages and in the spring attacked the monasteries of Jarrow and Tynemouth. Lindisfarne was their main target, but the monks being warned took their holy relics and the remnants of St. Cuthbert and fled for seven years. Finding little treasure, the Danes defaced ornaments and destroyed the monastery.

Danish raids continued in the 10th and 11th centuries. In 933 AD, the fortress at Bamburgh was raided by Danes and it was pillaged again in 1015.

In 1068, Newcastle was under attack by all sides, even, supposedly, their own!

Edgar the Etheling, heir to the crown of England; Malcolm King of Scotland and some Danish pirates invaded Monkchester (Newcastle). William the Conqueror overcame the raiders on Gateshead Fell, but almost levelled Monkchester to prevent it sheltering any of his enemies in the future.

Bamburgh Castle was built between 1894 and 1905. It stands on Whin Sill, an outcrop of basalt rock. The first castle on this site was probably built in the 6th century.

Rebellions

A rebel is someone who resists or rises in arms against an alleged rightful government, always a dangerous thing to do, and so it proved in 1569.

November 13th, 1569 – Rebels Routed

The Earls of Northumberland and Westmoreland with approximately 3,000 men marched on Durham. Their Catholic faith and concern for the Duke of Norfolk, imprisoned in the Tower for wanting to marry Mary Queen of Scots, instigated their rebellion. On entering Durham Cathedral they tore and trampled books of common prayer, English bibles and said Mass.

Some occupied Hartlepool, whilst Richard Norton led others south to Clifford Moor, near Wetherby. They mustered 600 horse and 4,000 foot in all.

However, at their rear, Sir George Bowes was raising forces against them and the Earl of Sussex was advancing with 3,000 men followed by the Earl of Warwick and his troops. The rebels retreated to Cumberland and the Earls fled to Scotland.

Retribution

The Earl of Northumberland, betrayed by a borderer, was executed on the scaffold at York. Sixty-three rebels were executed at Durham. Amongst them were an alderman called, Struther and a priest called Plumtree. Norton fled overseas; the Earl of Westmoreland died in Flanders many years later and some men offered their services to Spain. A number of the principals were pardoned, though the estates of those condemned as traitors were forfeit.

Rebelling against England's Elizabeth I was a dangerous business especially if a potential marriage placed you closer to the throne of Mary Queen of Scotland.

In 1715, twenty-seven years after James II and his family fled to France during the Glorious Revolution, his son James Francis Edward Stuart led a rebellion to regain the throne of Great Britain. The seeds of the rebellion lay in decisions made during the reigns of Henry VIII and Elizabeth I.

The Roman Catholic Question.

Henry VIII and Elizabeth I introduced the Protestant theology, but retained Roman Catholic ceremony in a new national church. It was supposed to be for all, but a minority held to the old faith in parts of Durham, Lancashire and Northumberland. The monarch was now the Head of State and Church and because Catholics were spiritually loyal to the Pope, they were regarded with suspicion.

In the 1630s, Charles I tried to be more tolerant towards Catholics whilst increasing his control of the apparatus of state, the courts and taxation. His autocratic monarchy caused a civil war and ended with his execution and the establishment of the Commonwealth, under Cromwell then his son Richard. The Commonwealth failed.

The eldest son of Charles I was then invited to become King. Unfortunately Charles II's leanings towards Catholics and tendency towards religious toleration didn't endear him to Parliament at the time. His attempts to become an absolute ruler and his negotiations with France didn't help either. He had no children with his wife Catherine of Braganza, so his brother James was his Catholic heir.

James II didn't really have a chance. He was generally unpopular because he believed in the Divine Right of Kings; wanted more religious freedoms for Catholics against the will of Parliament and was pro-French. The crisis point for many was when his son and heir James Francis Edward Stuart was born in June 1688. In November, a Newcastle mob let their feelings about James II become known.

The Mob and the Copper Statue

A little before the Glorious Revolution of 1689, Newcastle erected a copper statue which had two components: the base which was a horse on its hind legs and James II astride it. Standing on a white Italian marble pedestal on top of a black marble base in front of the Exchange, in Sandhill, Newcastle, it was sculpted by William Lawson and approved by Sir Christopher Wren, it cost Newcastle £800 sterling.

In November, 1688 Newcastle declared for William and Mary and a free Parliament. A mob dragged the statues of the king and his horse to the quay and threw them in the Tyne. They'd obviously no idea that copper would become very valuable metal in the 21st century! St. Andrews and All Saints parishes, however, requested the metal for a new bell and repairs to an old one.

With Parliament and public opinion against him, James II and his family fled to exile at St. Germain. In February, 1689, Parliament declared James II's flight meant he had abdicated and his daughter Mary and her husband William of Orange were invited to take the throne. The unintended consequence was that the exiled Stuarts at the Court of St. Germain and their disgruntled descendants were to become the focal point of Jacobite unrest for over fifty years.

Rebels with a cause have always given governments and crowned heads sleepless nights. The Jacobites involved in the rebellions of 1715 and the 1745 in particular must have given them nightmares. The word Jacobite comes from the Latin for King James Jacobus Rex. So Jacobites were followers of James II, his son James Francis Edward Stuart (the Old Pretender or Mr. Melancholy) in 1715 and his grandson Charles Edward Stuart (Bonnie Prince Charlie or the Young Pretender) in 1745.

Monument to James II, Sandhill, Newcastle. The inscription on the pedestal reads: 'James the II. By the Grace of God, of Great Britain, France and Ireland, King, Defender of the Faith, Sir William Creagh, Knight, Mayor, Samuel Gill, Esq., Sheriff, 1688.'

The '15

The '15 was caused by Scottish disenchantment with the Act of Union in 1707; resentment against the succession of the uncharismatic, Hanoverian George I; James Edward Stuart's ambition to restore the throne to the Stuarts, and the Earl of Mar, third secretary for Great Britain, who when publically snubbed by George I, sailed to Scotland to ignite the Jacobite rising. It failed.

The '45

George II had been on the throne since 1727 and by the late 1730s there appeared little threat from the Jacobites. However, several factors created the conditions for rebellion. There was a young figurehead for the Jacobites, Prince Charles Edward Stuart. The War of the Austrian Succession though unpopular in England, was very popular with the Jacobites because it meant France and Spain, two of their traditional supporters, were in conflict with England. An aborted French invasion of England in 1743 involving Prince Charles seemed to spur him into action. Using his own initiative and without French aid, he raised a rebellion and landed in Scotland in 1745.

The rebellion culminated in the Battle of Culloden in April, 1746 and the Jacobites lost. The government forces were led by Prince William, Duke of Cumberland who later earned the nickname 'Butcher Cumberland' because of his order of 'no quarter' for the defeated Jacobite army. The battle is important because it was the last battle fought on British soil.

The North, Scotland and the Stuarts

So what did the North of England have to do with Jacobites? Well, perhaps a lot more than you think. The North East has been described at this time as half being Roman

Catholic and the other half being very favourable towards it. In fact there were more staunch supporters of Catholicism in Northumberland and Durham than any other part of the country. They had influence among the highest echelons of the gentry as well as local Anglicans. The Bishop of Durham, the clergy and the local Anglican population actually protected their Roman Catholic friends and neighbours from the 1673 Test Act, which prevented those who refused to take the sacrament according to the rights of the Church of England, from holding military or civil office.

Northumberland and Durham were geographically closer to Scotland, than London. In rural areas there was a feudal system, perhaps similar to that of a laird and his tenants. And like Scotland, many in the North East resented interference from faraway London and its foreign monarchs, whether German or Dutch. There was certainly strong support in the area for the Stuarts during the Civil War.

When William of Orange (son of the Prince of Orange and Mary Stuart, daughter of Charles I) and his wife Mary (daughter of James II and Anne Hyde) were invited to share the throne in place of James II in 1689, their supporters were concerned there was little encouragement for their Cause in the North East. The area was a hotbed of Jacobite plotters whose intrigues and cause were to have severe repercussions in the years to come.

Jacobite Conspirators

The key conspirators were wealthy, influential and close to the throne. One was Sir John Fenwick of Wallington in Northumberland and his London house was a hub of Jacobite activity. He plotted to assassinate the King and take Newcastle. Not surprisingly, once captured, he was executed in 1697.

Edward Charlton of Hesleyside, Bellingham in Northumberland was another local Jacobite plotter. From 1689, his house in London was a nest for Jacobite spies who, as early as 1690, formulated a plan to invade England from the north east.

Other important Catholic families in Northumberland were supporters of the Jacobite cause: the Erringtons of Beaufront, the Haggerstones and the Swinburnes of Capheaton.

Plunder, Plans and Just Talk

In 1691, during the religious wars of the Grand Alliance against France, famous French Privateer Commander, Jean Bart, evaded an English blockade at Dunkirk and sailed towards Newcastle to attack shipping. Finding no ships he continued north and spotted Widdrington Castle in Northumberland.

One of his captains was a Scot called Melford or Mitford. Another traitor was Englishman Chetworth or Thetford, who acted as a pilot for the French by leading the ships: *Alcion, Aurore, Coute, Hereuse, Railleur, Seux* (?), *Sorciere* and *Tigre* into Druridge Bay. Thetford was caught in 1693, taken to Newgate, tried, found guilty and executed at Newcastle.

Claude De Forbin, was Bart's second in command and took charge of the landing party. Leaving 25 men to cover his retreat, he led the rest through the fields to pillage and set fire to Widdrington village, castle, barns, stables and outhouses. Lord Widdrington and his garrison were absent, fighting the Scots. Forbin apparently regretted the raid later, having discovered that the ornaments from the castle's private chapel were Catholic.

On their return journey the French torched the 16th century dower house (this housed the widow of an estate, thus allowing the male

The ruins of the preceptory and later dower house set on fire by a French landing party at Low Chibburn, Northumberland.

heir to live in the main house or castle). Part of the dower house used to be a preceptory first mentioned in 1313 and headquarters of the Knights Hospitaller of St. John.

Poorly equipped English cavalry and infantry arrived and killed one Frenchman who was carrying too much and had fallen behind his comrades. Forbin and the rest of his men made their way back to the waiting boats and the squadron. Before returning to France with his £6,000 worth of booty, Bart also burnt and scuttled some fishing boats.

The Court of St. Germain, home of Prince James (son of James II) also planned, with the support of local colliers and gentry, to land on the North East coast; seize Newcastle; invade England and Scotland and take London, fortunately it came to nought.

Despite the Act of Union in 1707 between England and Scotland, the rebellious link between Scotland and the north was a constant in Jacobite plans.

Jacobites in the North East were full of talk of using force of arms to restore James Stuart to the throne. Apart from an attempted French landing in Scotland by the French fleet in 1708, it may have appeared to be just talk.

The St. Germain Connection

Queen Anne succeeded to the throne in 1702, but it was only after 1710 that speculation about a Jacobite rising intensified. Amongst the most prominent of the conspirators was Catholic, James Radcliffe, 3rd Earl of Derwentwater, who was connected to the royal family through his mother (an illegitimate daughter of Charles II). He owned large estates in the north, was loyal to the Stuarts and educated at the Jesuit College of St. Louis le Grand in Paris.

Derwentwater and his brother Francis had spent their youth as companions to James Francis Edward Stuart at the Court of St. Germain. It is obvious where Derwentwater's loyalties lay as he was captured aboard a French ship in 1708, during a first attempt to recover the crown for James Stuart.

By 1709, Derwentwater settled in his northern estates and with another brother, Charles, and under the pretence of horse racing and bowls, proceeded to conspire for the Jacobite cause. Three years later, he married Catholic Anna Maria Webb, a supporter of the exiled Stuarts.

Another northerner who spent his youth at St. Germain was William, 4th Baron Widdrington, who lived at Stella, near Blaydon in County Durham. He was at the heart of the local Catholic community and had numerous mining interests.

1715 – The Derwentwater Disaster

Dilston Castle, on the far left was built by William Caxton in 1417. It was formerly the seat of James Radcliffe, Earl of Derwentwater. Lord's Bridge or Earl's Bridge (left) was probably erected around 1821 over Devil's Water and leads into Dilston Park which is 150 metres north-west of Dilston Hall.

The Old Pretender authorised the Earl of Mar to rise against the new English government, and the standard of rebellion was raised at Braemar in Scotland in September, 1715.

Derwentwater and Thomas Forster, one of the M.P.s for Northumberland proclaimed James Stuart, King of England and Scotland in Warkworth, Northumberland. Warkworth was the first place in England to do so.

Joined by some Scottish gentlemen, Derwentwater and Forster then went to Morpeth intending to surprise Newcastle with the knowledge that William Blackett, a wealthy Newcastle merchant and later mayor of Newcastle, was apparently a secret Jacobite and Tory and would support them. However, on learning that Newcastle was well defended, Derwentwater and Forster changed their minds and marched to Hexham and then on to Kelso to join Kenmur's Highlanders.

The rebellion failed after

Warkworth with boats on the River Coquet. The castle is in the background. Jon Cook from Newcastle, left 37 marks towards the building of the 14th century bridge.

Jacobite defeats at Sheriffmuir and Preston in November, 1715. Derwentwater and Forster were taken prisoner along with 75 other Englishmen, 145 Scottish noblemen and gentlemen and 1,300 ordinary soldiers. The most important prisoners were taken to London in a mock triumphal procession. One account talks of the mob being encouraged by well dressed citizens shouting insults and abuse at the Jacobites. The mob followed the procession derisively beating on warming pans as the prisoners were taken to Newgate, Marshalsea and other gaols.

The Jacobite prisoners were well treated and surprisingly given money, provisions and wine, and allowed visitors. Most of the Jacobites appeared to hope, that because they'd surrendered, they wouldn't be executed. However, when many of their friends were taken to trial and found guilty of high treason, their minds turned to escape.

James Radcliffe, Earl of Derwentwater

James Radcliffe, Earl of Derwentwater.

Derwentwater was 27 years old when, with William Gordon, Viscount Kenmore and Lord Nithsdale, he was sentenced to a traitor's death. Nithsdale was the only one to escape and did so by dressing in his wife's clothes.

On February 24th, 1716, Derwentwater wore a beaver hat with a broad brim and a drooping black plume; his wig was light flaxen and shoulder length, his hose were black and his clothes velvet. Black shoes with silver buckles encased his feet.

Derwentwater prayed and then addressed the crowd from the scaffold's railings. He praised the Pretender and apologised for pleading guilty to treason. This plea had accepted William and Mary's right to the throne. He went on to say this was disloyal to his lawful and rightful king, James II. In conclusion, he added, if he had been spared, he would have been honour bound not to take up arms again, against the reigning prince. He ended by saying he would die a Catholic.

The keeper of the Tower and the executioner appeared to be more interested in arguing about ownership of the Earl's wig and velvet clothes. Not surprisingly perhaps, the executioner won.

When Derwentwater was beheaded, his estates were forfeited and given to Greenwich Hospital. The county of Northumberland regarded him as a martyr.

Charles Radcliffe, Derwentwater's brother had also acted with Forster in the rebellion and was arraigned for treason. He refused to petition for mercy. After his brother, the Earl was executed, Charles was pardoned, but refused to accept it. He was detained in Newgate until December 1st, 1716, when he escaped.

He stubbornly continued to serve the exiled prince and in 1746 was given a naval commission by the King of France and was captured whilst in command of a ship carrying arms to the Jacobite rebels.

Taken to London, he was arraigned for his previous conviction. He denied the court's authority; produced his naval commission and stated he was a subject of the King of France and that he wasn't Charles Radcliffe, but the Earl of Derwentwater. The court wasn't impressed.

Derwent Reservoir, County Durham.

What he wore at his trial he also wore at the scaffold. He was described as being about fifty, five feet 10 inches tall, wearing a hat with a white feather, a bag-wig, a waistcoat with gold lace and a scarlet coat, with black velvet and gold buttons. He was beheaded on Tower Hill on December 8th, 1746.

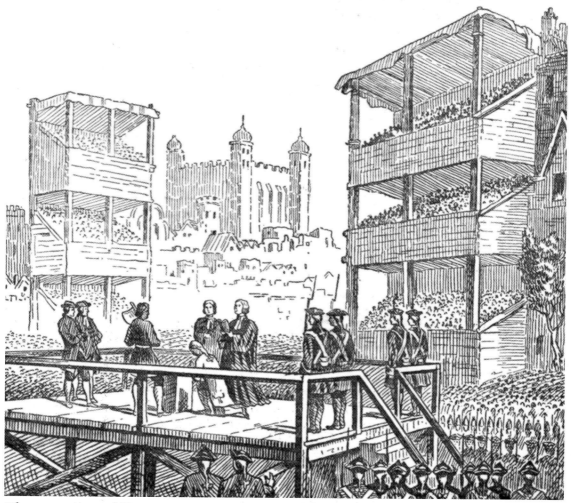

The execution of Derwentwater at Tower Hill on December 8th, 1746.

Forster Flees

Forster's trial was set for April 14th, 1716. His sister, Dorothy, visited him in London and cleverly made a wax impression of the key of his prison. A duplicate key was then smuggled to Forster and he escaped the night before the trial.

A proclamation for his capture offering a reward of £2,000 was immediately published. It described Forster as being overweight with stooped shoulders, having a fair complexion, grey eyes, large nose and wide mouth and speaking with a northern dialect.

Despite this, Forster wasn't captured, but was supposedly hidden in the Lord Crewe Arms in Blanchland, whilst a coffin full of sawdust was being buried at the church in Bamburgh attended by a *'grieving'* Dorothy.

He later fled to France, where he died in 1738. His body was brought to England and placed in the family crypt in St. Aidan's Church at Bamburgh.

Forster wasn't the only Jacobite prisoner to escape, nor was he the only one from Northumberland or with family connections there, that fought in the '15.

John Hall's case is particularly interesting. He was handsome and inherited an estate in North Tyne.

The 12th century Lord Crewe Arms, Blanchland.

Apparently his forwardness and indiscretions reduced its value. He married a gentlewoman from Newcastle without the consent of her father, Alderman Hutchinson. Hall moved to places like the Scottish borders and Hexham to put some distance between him and his father-in-law.

Through good husbandry and management, Hall stored his grain harvest in his barns and stock-yards. Unfortunately a fire broke out one night and burnt down his house, barns, stables containing horses, cow sheds and cows, and stacks of corn. He and his family narrowly escaped with their lives.

Thomas Forster.

When he moved to his own estate, with the expectation of a corn harvest, the weather turned against him. There was heavy rain, followed by flooding and a ruined harvest. These two unfortunate incidents were viewed as Hall's punishment for the previous deaths of two men.

Hall had heard about a quarrel between Mr. Fenwick and Mr. Septimus Forster M.P., but did nothing to prevent it. The sword fight took place in Newcastle and Mr. Forster was run through and died instantly. At Fenwick's trial, Hall gave evidence for him and was censured by the judge.

Later, when Hall was sitting at the bench of the Quarter Sessions, he got up and returned for his hat. He then wanted the Justices, the County Clerks and their books to be seized. This was refused. He later joined the rebels.

The rebels thought little of him and his short temper got him the nickname, *'Mad Jack Hall of Otterburn'.* He was executed at Tyburn on July 13th, 1716.
(Hexham Courant)

Was Forster hidden in a priest hole inside this fireplace in the Lord Crewe Arms, Blanchland?

England and Scotland share a border, yet even today we seem to have an uneasy alliance. In the middle of the 18th century the British government were obviously concerned that the Jacobite rebels, with French support, would invade England again After all, they'd seen it all before in 1715.

April 7th, 1745 – War and Rebellion
'War was declared on France. Daring French privateers were seen pursuing shipping close to Tynemouth bar.' (Mackenzie, 1827)

1745 – The Jacobites Are Coming
'Paid the gravedigger for concealing and securing the Church plate. £0. 5. 0.' (Charlton, R.J. Newcastle Town, p.188, from the records of All Saints)

Newcastle and the '45
On July 23rd, 1745, the Young Pretender landed on the Hebridean island of Eriskay and raised his standard at Glenfinnan on August 19th. The Prince leading a Jacobite army took Perth on September 5th and Edinburgh on the 16th.

The news of Sir John Cope's defeat by 2,500 Highlanders at Prestonpans on September 20th, 1745 arrived at Newcastle two days later. It was met with alarm as the Scots were only a few miles from Newcastle which had prospered since the last siege.

The *Newcastle Courant* of September 28th, 1745, recorded the preparations for the defence of the town when 600 Dutch troops entered Newcastle two weeks later to reinforce the, *'amateur garrison. Most of the volunteers were raw recruits and needed drilling.'*

One company wore, *'red and pink cockades'* and became particularly *'expert'* at drill. Cannon at nearly all towers and gates defended the town wall and, *'Sentry boxes were placed on the wall at intervals, and sandbags were suspended from the top of the wall to protect the stonework in case of attack.'* Stakes were placed in the shallow part of the river to stop any attempts to cross.

A proclamation signed by the Town Clerk stated:

October 12th, 1745

'Newcastle-upon-Tyne – All persons whatsoever residing without the walls of the said town that have any ladder or ladders, are desired immediately to bring the same into the town's yard behind the hospital in the Manors; and it is ordered that no person whatsoever (except the proper gunners) shall come near the great guns within the said town after six o'clock at night, and that no person whatsoever fire a gun or other firearms in or near the said town in the evening, and at night when it is dark, upon pain of imprisonment. And all persons living without the walls, but within the liberties of the said town, who have in their custody any firearms, are desired immediately to bring and deliver them at the mayor's house. And all persons living within the said town who have in their custody any pickaxes or shovels, are desired forthwith to deliver them at the same place. And notice is hereby given that the fair, customarily held on the 18th October, yearly, will not be held on the 18th instant, but sometime after, of which publick notice will be given – CUTHBERTSON.'

By October 24th a number of regiments were in the Newcastle area: *'Howard's (called the old Buffs), Ligonier's, Fleming's and Price's at Newcastle; Barrell's at South Shields; Monro's at North Shields; and Wolfe's* at Sunderland. A transport also arrived at Newcastle, with part of seven hundred Dutchmen, troops and eight transports at Berwick.'* (*Wolfe was later to become famous for defeating the French at Quebec.)

By the end of October, Marshal Wade was camped on Newcastle's Town Moor. The Jacobites sent a small detachment to deceive Wade into thinking their main force was marching on Newcastle, but instead took Carlisle. Wade went to Carlisle's aid, but got as far as Hexham when he heard Carlisle was in rebel hands.

The 'Old Castle', Newcastle.

There was national panic when Prince Charlie and his Highlanders reached Derby, a few days march from London. Despite having an army three times as large as the rebels, Wade didn't do battle, but returned to Newcastle as the Highlanders retreated.

The Battle of Culloden took place on April 16th, 1746. Colonel Stanwix in Newcastle received the news on April 21st: *'... it ran through the town like a torrent, and in a few minutes had extended to every corner. All business was immediately suspended, so that the streets were quickly crowded, and echoed with repeated shouts and acclamations; the bells of all the churches were rung, and the guns incessantly thundered from the ships and round the walls.'*

Cumberland arrived at Newcastle on the morning of July 23rd. He was, *'presented with the freedom of the town, in a gold box, by the mayor, and was also presented with the freedom of the company of the masters, mariners &c., of the Trinity House ... in another gold box ...'.* (Sykes, Vol. 1, p.173, 174, 182, 183)

Cumberland was then royally entertained.

Cruel Acts

It is always difficult to understand man's inhumanity to man. In 1301, Edward I of England's action against a countess was meant to humiliate, torture and warn.

1301 – The Caged Countess

Isabella MacDuff, the Countess-consort of Buchan, was the wife of John Comyn, Earl of Buchan. He sided with the English in the Wars of Scottish Independence and she allied herself to the Scots.

For reasons of safety, Isabella and Robert the Bruce's wife Elizabeth, daughter Marjory and sisters Christina and Mary were sent north, when Bruce was defeated in June 1306 at the Battle of Methven. Betrayed by the Earl of Ross, they were placed in the hands of Edward I of England. He ordered that Isabella be imprisoned in Berwick Castle and then suspended in the open air in an iron and stone cage as a warning to others. Apparently Mary Bruce was also placed in a similar cage outside Roxburgh Castle.

After four years Isabella was deposited in a Carmelite friary at Berwick, possibly because Bruce's support was growing and his relatives were valuable hostages.

Punishment can come in many forms and for the most unexpected reasons. What were Matilda Burgh and Margaret Usher doing in 1471?

1417 – Cross-dressing Crisis

Matilda Burgh and Margaret Usher were Peter Baxter's servants and lived in Newcastle. As women they were only legally allowed to get within a certain distance of the shrine of St. Cuthbert at Durham. They dressed as men, but were caught. Their punishment was to have a proclamation read about the penance and then to walk in male garments on the three festival days at the head of the procession in St. Nicholas' Church and on three other holidays, at the church of All Saints in Newcastle. Their employers had to attend Durham's spiritual court as they had been charged with being, *'counsellors and abettors'* in the deed. (*Sykes, Vol. 1, p.57-58*)

Matida and Margaret may have felt liberated when dressed as men, but when discovered would have been treated with derision. It really didn't do, to dress or act outside of the accepted norm; Jo. Servant found this out to his cost in 1633.

March 4th, 1633 – Married or Not?

Mr. Flood, a Roman Catholic priest, presided over a secret religious ceremony in which Jo. Servant was married to Jane Pickney in Crossgate. However, it was regarded as a sham wedding at the time and Servant had to stand at the Market Cross and make a public *'penitential confession'* at Durham's Market Cross as well as pay a fine of £40! (*Sykes, Vol. 1, p.88*)

Poor William Collingwood just wanted to keep what he owned.

Collingwood's Conundrum

In the early 17th century, William Collingwood from Kemmerston, Ford, lived in the borders which were basically under martial law and ravaged by reivers (lawless men). Finding his horse had been stolen, Collingwood eventually caught the Scottish thief and recovered his now weary horse a year later.

Having deposited the Scot in Berwick, Collingwood must have congratulated himself for a job well done as he could now seek recompense from the thief for his horse. Unfortunately the Scot escaped!

Reivers would have thought little of Collingwood's troubles. They lived and farmed amongst those they stole from and often 'borrowed' useful animals that could pull a plough or cart. It made sense, letting the animal loose, once it had been worked hard, so the owner fed it and got it fit again.

Of course if Collingwood hadn't wanted to be robbed in the first place, then all he had to do was pay the reivers 'rent' or blackmail (a word they invented by the way). Such was the reivers' logic.

What logic drove John Brown and Christopher Richardson in the 18th century to do away with their master?

Attempted Murder

In August, 1725, butler and gardener, John Brown and Christopher Richardson, tried to poison their master, William Coatsworth, Esq., from Park House, Gateshead. They put arsenic in his chocolate. Having been found guilty at the Durham Assizes, one was to be confined for five years and the other three. Annually on the tenth of June, they were whipped ten times round the market place and had to stand in the pillory every Saturday after the quarter sessions for peace.

Park House, Gateshead. It still stood in 1974, part of the Clarke, Chapman-John Thompson Engineering Works.

Women were also at risk when unaccompanied, as the two incidents below illustrate:

Soldiers Two

In September 1756, two soldiers attacked a young woman near the windmill on Gateshead Fell. They tried to take her clothes and other belongings. As they couldn't do this quietly they decided to throw her down an ancient coal pit, about 20 yards in depth. She wasn't found until seven days later. Fortunately, she hadn't been hurt in the fall and had cleverly used her shoe to catch rain water, which she drank.

A Blackguard

Elizabeth Whatoff, alias Charlton, was robbed on August 20th, 1725. A pistol was fired and such violent offences committed against her that she should have died. At his trial, it was revealed that bigamist Thomas Charlton of Birtley, Northumberland had persuaded Elizabeth to marry him. His defence was that he couldn't get rid of her and had been forced into the marriage. He was found guilty of robbery and bigamy and executed at Durham.

A child's first defence against the cruelties of others is his or her parents. If they didn't care; were starving or dead and the child placed in unscrupulous hands, then anything could happen.

October, 1735 – Unusual Winnings

'A child of James and Elizabeth Leesh, of Chester-le-Street, was played for at cards, at the sign of the salmon, one game, four shillings against the child, by Henry and John Trotter, Robert Thompson and Thomas Ellison, which was won by the latter, and delivered to them accordingly.' (Sykes, Vol.1, p.151)

Might is Right?

One way to solve a disagreement between two gentlemen was a duel. Duelling has always been illegal in England as it was viewed as a breach of the peace and the survivor and seconds could be charged with manslaughter or murder.

The first recorded duel in England was between William Count of Eu and Godfrey Baynard in 1096; one of the last was in Wimbledon, England when Captain Tuckett apparently libelled Lord Cardigan in 1840. Cardigan wounded Tuckett and won! Newcastle also had its duels as seen in the two incidents below.

August 7th, 1637 – A Duel

A duel fought at Whitehall Dyke Nook. Mr. John Trollop the younger was convicted of killing William Selby, Esquire of Newcastle. At the assizes at Durham, Mr. Trollop was outlawed.

August 6th, 1638 – Trial by Combat?

Ralph Claxton, demandant, and Richard Liliburne, tenant, were in dispute about the rights of land at Thickley and had agreed to trial by waging battle.

At 10 o'clock at the assizes, Judge Berkley of Durham was presented with Claxton's champion, George Cheney, with stave and sandbag. Cheney threw down a gauntlet with five coins in it. Liliburne then produced his champion, William Peverell, who did exactly the same.

The judge ordered two bailiffs to take the champions into custody till eight o'clock next morning.

Eventually Charles I intervened and asked the northern circuit judges to decide how the dispute could be tried another way. The judges overruled Justice Berkley's argument that Liliburne was entitled to a trial by battle. The trial was deferred from year to year until a bill was brought to abolish this, 'mode of decision.'

Thank goodness Charles I had some common sense. However, in 1869 there didn't seem to be a lot of it around.

1869 – Schoolmaster Shoots Boy

Thomas Hodkinson was a schoolmaster who lived with his son in Walker, a peaceful parish of Long Benton. On the morning of the March 25th, Mr. Worden, a bookseller in Gray Street, Newcastle, had called in the bailiffs to seize Hodkinson's goods in lieu of money owed. This attracted the attention of a large number of boys. According to the prosecution, the boys made little noise whilst running around the garden in front of Mr. Hodkinson's house from 7.20am-8.00am. Five windows in Hodkinson's house were broken, but not from outside. It appears Hodkinson or his son had smashed them with a pole.

Walker Quay in the 19th century.

Hodkinson's Trial

Robert Widdrington, assistant to Mr. Worden, stated in front of Mr. Justice Hayes and a jury that he hadn't seen the prisoner till half an hour after he arrived. There was a crowd outside as well as about fifty boys. He'd said, *'Mr. Hodkinson, you had better let me in and have no more unpleasantness.'* It was pointed out that Hodkinson was already distressed as Widdrington's master, Mr. Worden, had been outside his home all night. Widdrington went on to say that he saw a number of boys carrying sticks and hissing and shouting at the bailiffs. They didn't throw any stones.

Widdrington said Hodkinson had blamed him for the fracas when he stated, *'You are the cause of all this.'* Widdrington replied, *'I was not the cause of the mischief – far from it.'*

Three boys were in the garden when Hodkinson apparently threatened to *'blow some of the lads' brains out'* with a loaded pistol, if they didn't leave the garden.

Widdrington told him, *'... shoot me not the boys.'* Hodkinson appeared to point the muzzle through a broken pane, at Widdrington, but then turned the pistol and shot a 15 year old boy called Robert Hughes.

When questioned, Hughes, from Chapel Street, Walker explained that he'd left work at half past seven, knew Hodkinson's house and saw the boys outside. He said there were a lot of people, but they weren't doing anything. He didn't see any stones thrown or windows broken. After twenty minutes he heard Hodkinson tell the *'bum'* he'd *'blow his brains out.'* The *'bum'* replied, *'Fire at me, but don't fire at the boys.'*

Hodkinson turned the gun on Hughes and shot him in the thighs and chest. When examined Hughes was found to have over fifteen small shot wounds in his body, some had, *'penetrated an inch and a half ...'*

Sergeant Pike examined the railings which were 50ft from the house's windows and found *'eleven shot marks'* which were an inch in depth. He arrested Hodkinson and charged him with, *'shooting with intent to murder'*. Hodkinson replied that, *'the boys would not leave the window. When I told them to go away they threw stones at me. My son told me there was no shot in the pistol'*. On searching Hodkinson's house, the sergeant found some books, marbles, powder and a box of percussion caps in a drawer. Sergeant Amos found the pistol in Hodkinson's house.

It appears that whilst trying to gain access to the house, the bailiffs stopped provisions and beer entering as they tried to smoke out Hodkinson and his son. When questioned, Widdrington said Mr. Worden hadn't tried to *'stink'* Hodkinson out by pouring chemicals down his chimney, but Worden had used straw and sacking, as ordered by the bailiff, *'to smoke him out'.*

The defence used the arguments that any man who was besieged by bailiffs would feel *'indignant'*; that the bailiffs were not justified in the actions they took as

A Tyneside police sergeant.

Hodkinson's debts were not due for collection and that there was *'no proof of intent to injure.'* The jury, after a short discussion found Hodkinson, *'Not guilty.'* He was congratulated by his friends as he left the court.

(*The Newcastle Courant, April 16th, July 23rd, 1869; Reynolds Newspaper (London), Sunday, July 25th, 1869*)

Penal Servitude
On the Trail of Ann Thompson

The story of Ann Thompson illustrates the difficulties of historical research. I started with one Ann Thompson and ended up with three! They'd all committed similar crimes, had been convicted around the same time and were transported to Australia.

It is possible to tentatively trace convicts from birth, conviction and sentence, to eventual freedom or death if the records allow. However, it was in the felons' interests to conceal their past by changing their name or other facts. After painstaking research in England and Australia one Ann Thompson was discounted as her place of origin appeared to be Liverpool. This is what genealogists discovered about the other two. The first Ann Thompson was born in Carlisle. Her offences, of pick-pocketing/larceny in Newcastle, were recorded in several places.

1839 – The First Ann Thompson

NEWCASTLE POLICE OFFICE, MANORS
'*Saturday, February 10th – Before Mr. Aid, SPEDDING Mr. Justice Plummer. Eliza Hill was brought up on a charge of picking the pocket of John Wright, of a silver watch, but was discharged on account of the contradictory evidence of the prosecutor. Eleanor Chandler & Ann Thompson were brought up and discharged for a similar offence to the above.'*

Newcastle Courant, Friday March 8th, 1839
Newcastle Spring Assizes
'*Tuesday March 5th. Crown Court – before Mr. Baron Alderson. The learned justice took his seat in the town court shortly after nine o'clock this morning.*

ANN THOMPSON (35) was convicted on a charge of having, on the 7th day of February, stolen a sovereign, a pencil case, a clasp knife, and a pair of woollen gloves from the person of Timothy Halleran, in a crowd; and the prisoner having been several times summarily convicted before the magistrates, she was sentenced to be transported for 10 years.'

The Northern Liberator, Saturday March 9th, 1839
'*ANN THOMPSON was indicted for stealing one pencil, a pair of gloves, and a sovereign, from Timothy Halloran, on the night of the 7th February.*

Timothy Halloran stated that on going up Pilgrim Street on the night in question, the prisoner came and thrust her hand into his pocket; he immediately searched and found she had stolen a sovereign out of his pocket; he detained her and gave her into custody; subsequently he found that she had also stolen from him a pencil and a pair of gloves. A policeman corroborated this evidence.'

Guilty. Transported for ten years.'

So what happened to this Ann? Well, she was transported on the *Hindostan* which sailed from London on May 9th, 1839 and arrived in Van Dieman's Land (now Tasmania) on September 12th, 1839.

A chain gang in Van Dieman's Land.

A host of information about each prisoner was compiled in volumes entitled 'Indents'. For instance Ann's physical description, along with that of every other convict, was recorded when she was checked for identifying marks before she disembarked. Ann would have been stripped to the waist and physically examined. She was described as having a high forehead, long face and broad chin. Her hair was brown, eyes hazel and complexion dark. It was also noted that her mouth was large; she had a missing lower tooth and was 5ft 2ins tall without her shoes. Her trade was probably that of a house maid or housekeeper.

On arrival after 1841, each convict made a statement or confession for the offence he or she had committed and this information was copied onto a Conduct Record. Ann's Conduct Record was difficult to decipher, but her life as a convict seems to have been made worse by extra punishments:

Ann Thompson

Prisoner number: *154.*

Arrival: *Hindostan* on September 11, 1839.

Convicted: Northumberland, Newcastle upon Tyne Assizes.

Date of conviction: March 10, 1839.
'Transported for larceny from the Prison Gaol report. Bad in temper ... imprisoned 10 times before surgeon report ... stated this offence stealing money from Timothy Allen once for a boat ... several times for being disorderly ... married and 1 ch. Husband, John ... in this town.'

May 19, 1840 Being Drunk.

May 28, 1840 Drunk, 10 days Sol.

June 24, 1840 Drunk ... Sol.

August 7, 1841 Drunk in a public street yesterday, 14 days.

November 1841 Absent without leave, 1 month ...

February 2 1842 ... Drunk and insolent yesterday, 3 months hard labour, Crime Class.

June 22 1842 Drunk 6 days.

Key: ch – child   Sol – solitary

It sounds as if Ann drank a lot, possibly to forget her misery. Sadly, her paper trail trickles out at this point.

A wagonway in Tasmania where convicts provided the 'power'.

April 7th, 1841 – The Second Ann Thompson

This Ann Thompson was probably born in Writon, Cumberland in 1819. She would have been in her early twenties when shipmaster, William Colling, accused her of theft. Sentenced at Newcastle upon Tyne Quarter Sessions on April 7th, 1841, her case was recorded in the *Newcastle Courant*:

'Ann Thompson was convicted of stealing a purse ... From the person William Colling, a shipmaster, from Sunderland ... Colling arrived from Sunderland and went in the Brandy Butt in the Side; here the prisoner came to him and told him she was in a state of starvation and soliciting charity. Moved by her story the prosecutor gave her a shilling and she brought in some bread and cheese. They remained together for a short time longer, and the prosecutor then moved to leave the house, but as he was doing this Thompson beckoned up the staircase and began to talk. The conversation was, however speedily put an end to by the abrupt departure of the prisoner and as soon as Colling had recovered from the 'fluster' which the circumstances had thrown him he found that he was minus his purse and his money.

The police were made acquainted with the affair, and in the afternoon of the same day, the prisoner was apprehended in a state of intoxication, in Sandgate. She had some money in her hand at the time, and it further turned out...she had employed the few hours between the robbery and her transfer to the prison a metamorphoss (sic) of her outer person. Various shopkeepers swore to having sold her and another girl articles ... and items of dress during the hours in question.

A previous conviction of felony was proven against her.

Ten years transportation.'

Sunderland in the early 1800s.

Was Ann starving or was this just a ruse to gain Colling's sympathy and then trust? What was the '*fluster*' on the staircase? Was Colling telling the truth? The answers are lost in the past, but we can trace Ann's footsteps and find out what happened to her. She was taken to London and on June 23rd, 1841 was transported on the *Garland Grove* to Van Dieman's Land where she landed on October 10th, 1841.

Although sentenced to 10 years, Ann actually served almost 12 years, of which approximately 3 years 4 months were hard labour. Her Conduct Report gives us a good idea of what her life was like:

Ann Thompson

Prison Number: 179

Arrival: *Garland Grove* October 10, 1841

Date of conviction: Newcastle upon Tyne April 7, 1841
'*Transported for Larceny from the prison and previous Correction Gaol report very dishonest and – before – Stated this offence Stealing money for … being disorderly – 2 years in the town – Report Good.*'

October 22, 1841: Absent without leave, 6 days – solitary.

January 12, 1842: Absent without leave and drunk.

February 12, 1842: Absent 2 days and nights without leave, 6 months hard labour in separate working cells.

April 23, 1842: Absconding, 6 months hard labour in the separate working cell.

November 31, 1842: Disobedience, violent dumb insolence, 6 months hard labour.

May 15, 1844: Drunk and disorderly, 3 months hard labour in H. of C.

May 31, 1844: Approved. Insubordination, 12 months hard labour…to be kept separate.

June 17, 1845: Absent without leave, 1 month hard labour …

July 11, 1845: Drunk, absent without leave, 2 months hard labour.

January 23, 1846: Absent without leave … Factory Hobart.

November 18, 1846: Absent without leave … Factory Hobart.

November 11, 1846: Out after hours, 1 month hard labour, the Factory.

March 10, 1847: … and labour.

June 25, 1847: Absconding … to be passed separately …

July 31, 1847: Absent without leave, 2 months hard labour.

April 5, 1853: Free Certificate.

Key: H of C. – House of Correction

When given her Certificate of Freedom on April 5th, 1853 Ann had survived a brutal prison regime. However, there are twists in the rest of her tale. If her birth date and age when transported are correct, then she should have been 30 years old when she married Joseph Ashbury in Fingal, Tasmania and 34 years old when freed. One record states that she married when she was 24 years old and another reveals she used two surnames 'Thomas/ Thompson'. Why?

Record of Marriage

Marriage: Ann Thomas/Thompson Garland Grove married Joseph Ashbury Westmorland

Date of decision – Appd prison –

– *satisfied late for the – as to the death of his former wife.*
– *Married January 22nd, 1849 by the Reverend Mr. Richardson.*

Ann's husband, Joseph, was a convict from Worcester who had been sentenced to transportation for life. He was apparently 37 years old when he married her.

The couple appear not to have had any children as there are none listed or registered in the baptismal records. It would be nice to think that after all their hardships, Ann and Joseph found some happiness at last. Unfortunately, this account of a trial appeared in the local paper about 22 years later:

> *'Tried SC Hobart 21st November 1871 (as Ann Ashbury) feloniously receiving stolen articles (Two years imprisonment)'* (*Hobart Mercury*)

Joseph, died on May 9th, 1876 at Oatlands, Tasmania when he should have been 64 years of age. The irony is that Tasmania Pioneer Records (Reg. No. 35) state he was 75! Did Ann and Joseph both lie to each other about their ages? As of today we have no record of Ann's death.

Conclusion

Deaths, disasters and dastardly deeds have always been with us. It says something about the human spirit that most people, who have suffered the worst life, the elements and fellow human beings can throw at them, refuse to be bowed and carry on.

More flooding – this time at South Church, Bishop Auckland. But these children do not seem to mind!

Picture Credits

Summerhill Books would like to thank the following who kindly gave us images to use in this publication:

Chris Bartley, Steve Boundey, Alan Brett, John Carlson, Philip Curtis, George Nairn, Nicola Smith and Sharyn Taylor.

Bibliography

Beckensall, S. (2005). Northumberland Shadows of the Past, Tempus Publishing Limited, Great Britain.

Collings, P. (–). The Illustrated Dictionary of North-East Shipwrecks, Collings & Brodie, Co. Durham.

Foxe, J. (1570). Actes and Monuments, John Dey, London.

Hansard, T. C. (1819). The Parliamentary Debates From the Year 1803 to the Present Time: Forming A Continuation of the Work Entitled 'The Parliamentary History of England from the Earliest Period to the Year 1803' Vol. XLI Comprising the Period From the Twenty-Third Day of November, 1819 To the Twenty-Eight Day of February, 1820, Parliament, London.

Keys, D. and Smith, K. (2006). Tales from the Tyne, Tyne Bridge Publishing, Newcastle upon Tyne.

Landells, S. (2010). Rescues in the Surf – The story of the Shields lifeboats 1789-1939, Tyne Bridge Publishing, Newcastle upon Tyne.

Mackenzie & Dent. (1810). A Historical and Descriptive View of the County of Northumberland and of The Town and County of Newcastle upon Tyne with Berwick-upon-Tweed and other celebrated Places on the Scottish Border ...' (Vol. II), Mackenzie and Dent, Newcastle upon Tyne.

Mallinson, A. (2011). The Making of the British Army From the Civil War to the Reign of Terror, Bantam Books, London.

Morgan, A. (2007). Victorian Panorama, City of Newcastle upon Tyne Libraries and Information Service, Tyne Bridge Publishing, Newcastle upon Tyne.

Patten, R. (1745). The History of the Rebellion in the year 1715, III Edition, James Roberts, Warwickshire, London.

Phillips, M. (1894). A History of Banks, Bankers, & Banking in Northumberland, Durham and Yorkshire, Illustrating the Commercial Development of the North of England From 1755 to 1894, With Numerous Portraits, Facsimiles of Notes, Signatures, Documents, &, Effingham, Wilson & Co, Royal Exchange, London.

Sadler, J. (2005). Border Fury England and Scotland at War 1296-1568, Pearson Education Limited, Great Britain.

Sloane, B. (2011). The Black Death in London, The History Press, Stroud, Gloucestershire.

Smith, K and J. (2008). The Great Northern Miners, Tyne Bridge Publishing, Newcastle upon Tyne.

Sykes, J. (1866). Local Records; or, Historical Events, Which Have Occurred in Northumberland and Durham, Newcastle-upon-Tyne, and Berwick-upon-Tweed, From the Earliest Period of Authentic Record to the Present Time; with Biographical Notices of Deceased Persons of Talent, Eccentricity and Longevity. (Vol. I and II), T. Fordyce, Newcastle.

Talbot, B. (2007). Alice in Sunderland, Jonathan Cape, London.

Tegner, H. (1968). The long Bay of Druridge, Frank Graham, Newcastle upon Tyne.

Wilson, (1966). Wilson's Handbook to Morpeth and Neighbourhood, Newgate Press, Morpeth.

Newspapers

Blyth Bi News
Blyth News
Daily Mail – August 19th, 2011, p.20.
Hexham Courant
Hobart Mercury (Australia) – November 21st, 1871.
Illustrated Weekly London News – June, 20th, 23rd, 1883
Monthly Chronicle of North-Country Lore and Legend, 1887
Newcastle Chronicle
Newcastle Courant
Newcastle Journal
Otago Witness – Issue 1987 – March 24th, 1892, p.20.
Reynolds Newspaper (London) – July 25th, 1869.
Sunderland Echo – June 13th, 2008
The Graphic – June 23rd, 1883
The Northern Liberator – March 9th, 1839
The Times – June 18th, July 3rd, July 5th, 1883
Wansbeck Telegraph

Reports

Leifchild, J.R. (1842). 'The Employment of Children and Young Persons in the Collieries, Lead Mines and Iron Works of Northumberland and the North of Durham; and on the Condition, Treatment, and Education of such Children and Young Persons.'

Websites

www.fiddlersgreen.net/models/aircraft/Balloon-Lunardi.html
www.londonguide.co.uk/london
www.ultimatehistoryproject.com/fads
www.cmhrc.co.uk/cms/document/1842_N_bland.pdf
www.visitsouthtyneside.co.uk/article/12650/historicbuildings-and-monuments
www.tynelives.org.uk/lifetxt/watch.htm
www.sunderland.gov.uk/CHHpHandler.ashx?id = 6964& = 0
www.searlecanada.org/sunderland/sunderland011.html#londontimes
www.ndfhs.co.ukarticles/hexhamriot.hmtl
www.ramsdale.org/militia.htm
www.bbc.co.uk/health/physical/health/conditions/cholera.html

Australian Sources

New South Wales and Tasmania, Australia Convict Musters, 1806-1849 Original data: Home Office Settlers and Convicts, New South Wales and Tasmania; (The National Archives Microfilm Publication HO10, Pieces 5, 19-20, 32-51); The National Archives of the UK (TNA), Kew, Surrey, England.

(1.) Ann Thompson – New South Wales Convict Musters, 1806-1849, Ledger Returns S-Z; Year: 1846, Source Citation: Class: HO 10, Piece: 39; DESCRIPTION LISTS OF FEMALE CONVICTS, Series Number: CON19, Start Date 01 Oct 1828 End Date 31 Dec 1853; TA60 CONVICT DEPARTMENT 01 Jan 1818-31 Dec 1877, Item Number: CON15/ 1/9, Start Date: 12 Sept 1839 End Date 1839, Location: HOB, Copy Number: Z2517; CON15 INDENTS OF FEMALE CONVICTS 09, Start Date: May 1831 End Date: 24 Feb 1853; TA60 CONVICT DEPARTMENT 01 Jan 1818-31 Dec 1877.

(2.) Ann Thompson – Australian Convict Transportation Registers – Other Fleets & Ships, 1791-1868, Source Citation: Class: HO 11, Piece: 12; Australia Marriage Index, 1788-1950, Registration number: 84; Tasmanian Archives Site, Conduct Record: CON40/1/10; Description List: CON19/1/3; CONDUCT REGISTERS OF FEMALE CONVICTS CON40/1/10 Surnames S-Y; Copy Number: Z2590; Series CON40 CONDUCT REGISTERS OF FEMALE CONVICTS ARRIVING IN THE PERIOD OF THE ASSIGNMENT SYSTEM 01 Jan1803-31 Dec 1843; CONVICT PERMISSION TO MARRY RECORDS, CON52/1/3 P 1, RGD37/8: 1849/84; Tasmania Pioneer Marriage Record, Reg. No.37, Year 1849; Tasmania Pioneer Deaths Record, Reg. No. 35, Year 1876.

Also available from Summerhill Books

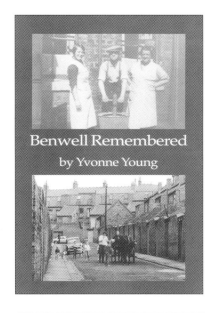

Benwell Remembered
by Yvonne Young

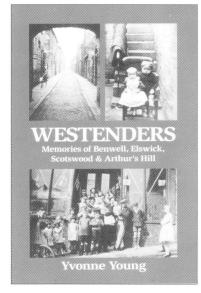

WESTENDERS
Memories of Benwell, Elswick, Scotswood & Arthur's Hill

Yvonne Young

Benwell, Buses & Boxing
The Story of Audrey Guthrie

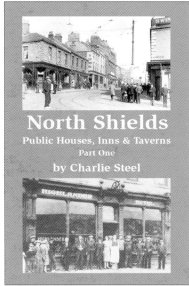

North Shields
Public Houses, Inns & Taverns
Part One
by Charlie Steel

Wallsend Remembered
Looking back at growing up in Wallsend, Howdon & Willington Quay

by Steve Boundey

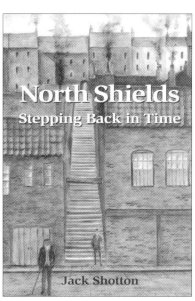

North Shields
Stepping Back in Time

Jack Shotton

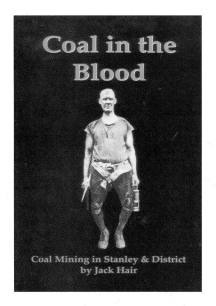

Coal in the Blood
Coal Mining in Stanley & District
by Jack Hair

TOMMY ARMSTRONG
THE PITMAN POET
BY RAY TILLY
GRANDSON OF TOMMY

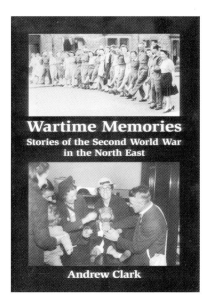

Wartime Memories
Stories of the Second World War in the North East

Andrew Clark

www.summerhillbooks.co.uk